George Stubbs:
102 Paintings and Drawings

By Maria Tsaneva

First Edition

*****

I0474608

George Stubbs: 102 Paintings and Drawings
*****

Foreword

George Stubbs (1724 – 1806) was an outstanding English
animal painter and anatomical draftsman, best known for
his paintings of horses. Stubbs also painted a wide variety of
other animals, including the lion, tiger, giraffe, monkey, and
rhinoceros, which he was able to observe in private
menageries. According to the artist Ozias Humphrey, Stubbs
was so convinced of the importance of observation that he
visited Italy in 1754 only to reinforce his belief that nature is
superior to art. Among Stubbs's best-known pictures are
several depicting a horse being frightened or attacked by a
lion (Horse Frightened by a Lion, 1770) in which he
emphasizes the wild terror of the former and the predatory
power of the latter.
Stubbs's historical paintings are among the least successful
of his works; much more convincing are his scenes of
familiar country activities done in the 1770s. Unfortunately,
he tended to execute his paintings in thin oil paint, and
relatively few survive in undamaged condition. His last
years were spent on a final work of anatomical analysis: A
Comparative Anatomical Exposition of the Structure of the
Human Body, with that of a Tiger and Common Fowl, for
which he completed 100 drawings and 18 engravings.
Stubbs was born in Liverpool, the son of a currier and
leather merchant. Information on his life up to age thirty-
five is sparse, relying almost entirely on notes made by
fellow artist Ozias Humphry towards the end of Stubbs's
life.

Stubbs worked at his father's trade until he was 15 or 16, and after his father's death in 1741 was briefly apprenticed to a Lancashire painter and engraver named Hamlet Winstanley. He soon left as he objected to the work of copying to which he was set. Thereafter as an artist he was self-taught. In the 1740s he worked as a portrait painter in the North of England and from about 1745 to 1751 he studied human anatomy at York County Hospital. He had had a passion for anatomy from his childhood, and one of his earliest surviving works is a set of illustrations for a textbook on midwifery which was published in 1751.

In 1754 Stubbs visited Italy. Forty years later he told Ozias Humphry that his motive for going to Italy was, "to convince himself that nature was and is always superior to art whether Greek or Roman, and having renewed this conviction he immediately resolved upon returning home". In 1756 he rented a farmhouse in the village of Horkstow, Lincolnshire, and spent 18 months dissecting horses, assisted by his common-law wife, Mary Spencer.[2] He moved to London in about 1759 and in 1766 published The anatomy of the Horse. The original drawings are now in the collection of the Royal Academy.

Even before his book was published, Stubbs's drawings were seen by leading aristocratic patrons, who recognised that his work was more accurate than that of earlier horse painters such as James Seymour, Peter Tillemans and John Wootton. In 1759 the 3rd Duke of Richmond commissioned three large pictures from him, and his career was soon secure. By 1763 he had produced works for several more dukes and other lords and was able to buy a house in Marylebone, a fashionable part of London, where he lived for the rest of his life. His last project A Comparative Anatomical Exposition of the Structure of the Human Body was left unfinished upon Stubbs's death at the age of 81 on 10 July 1806, in London.

Paintings, Drawings and Etchings

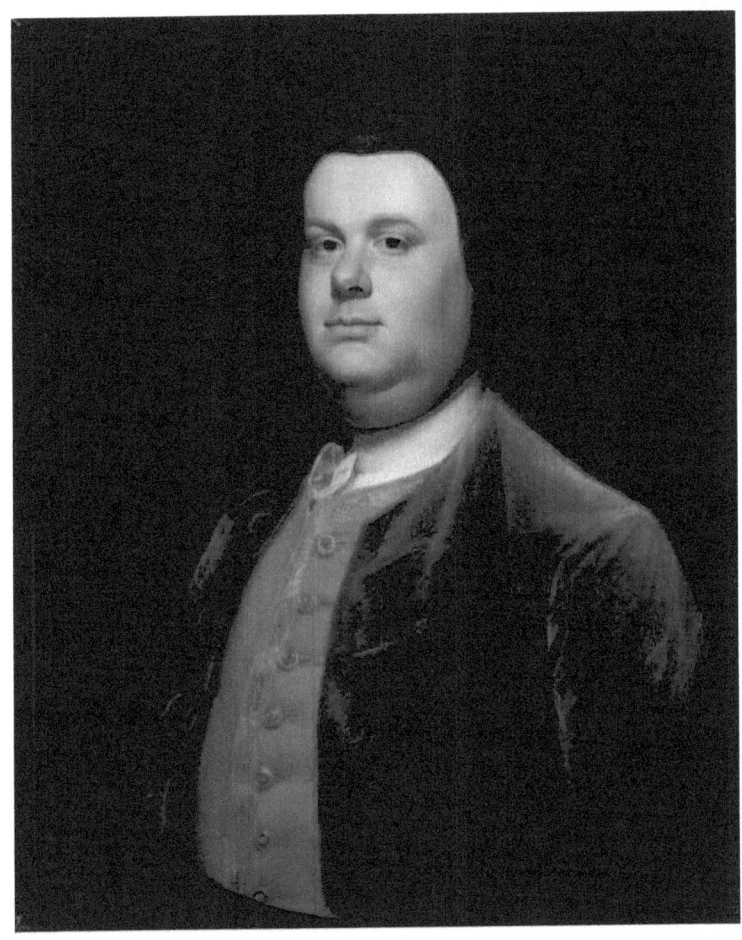

James Stanley, 1755, Oil on canvas

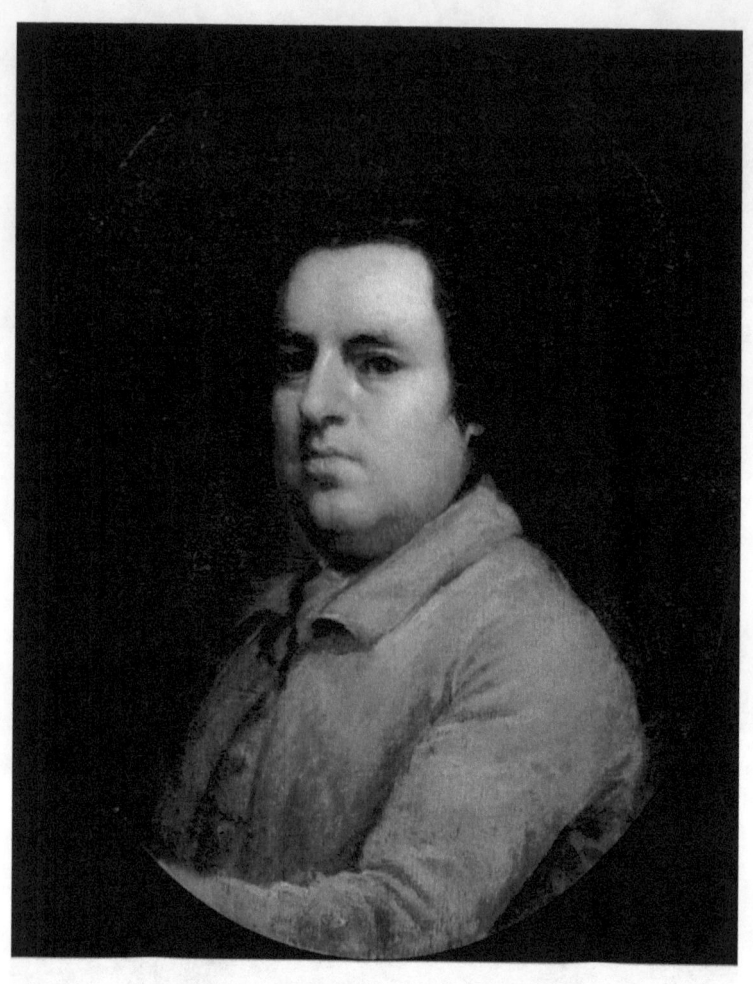

Self-Portrait, 1759, Oil on copper

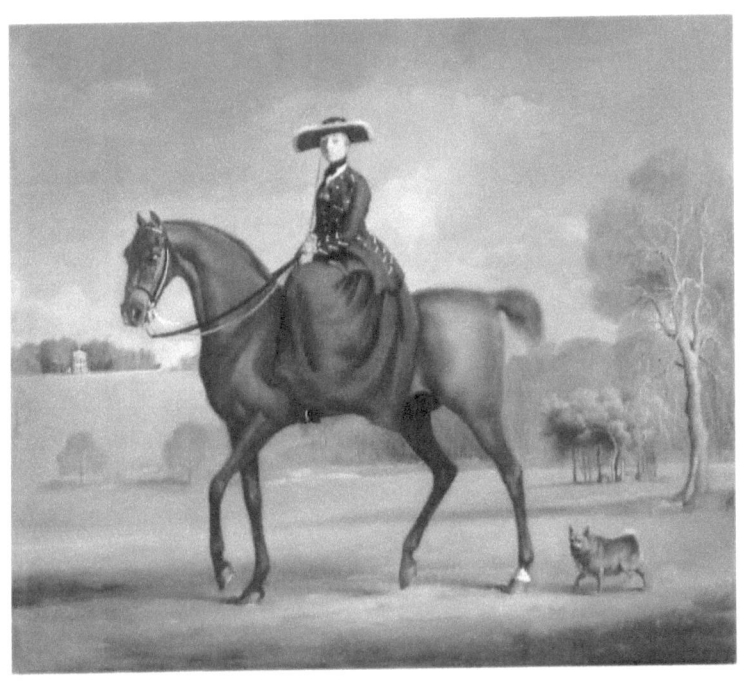

The Countess of Coningsby in the Costume of the
Charlton Hunt, 1760, oil on canvas

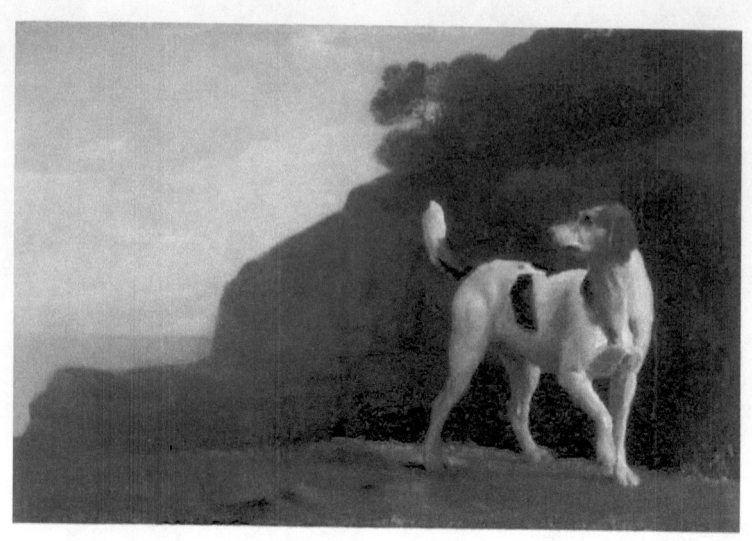

Foxhound, 1760, oil

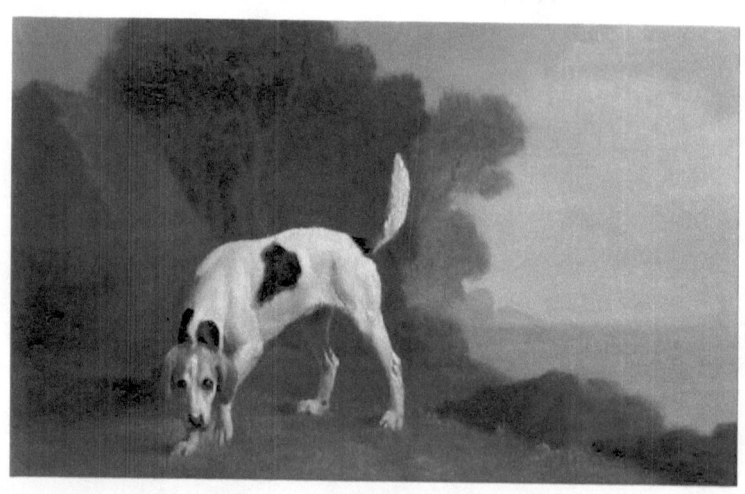

Foxhound, 1760, oil

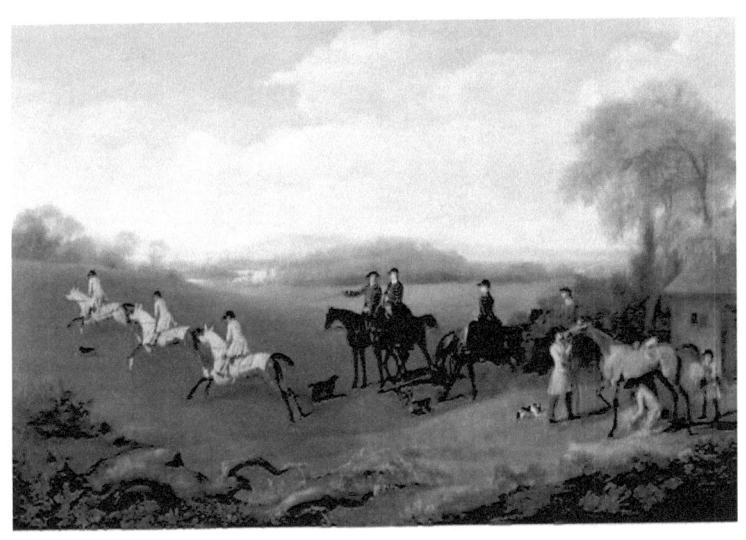

Racehorses Belonging to the Duke of Richmond
Exercising at Goodwood, 1760-1761, oil on canvas

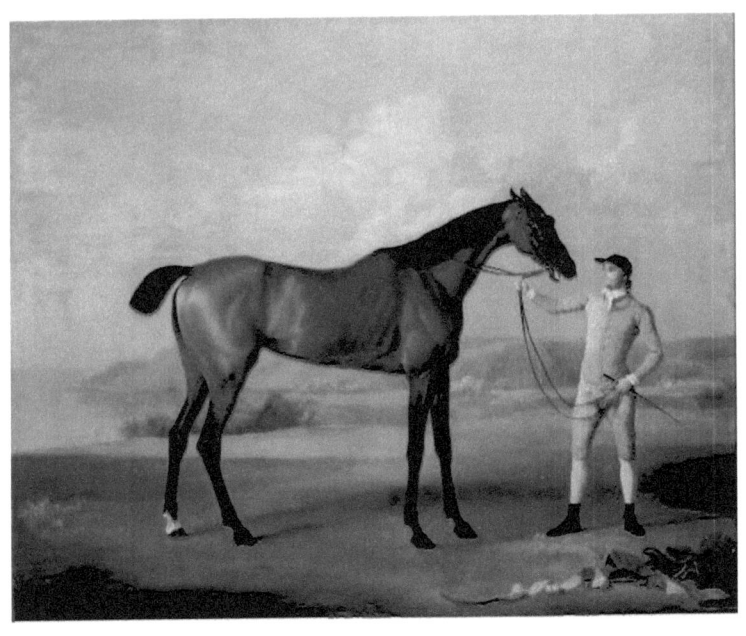

Molly Long-legs with her Jockey, 1761-1762, oil

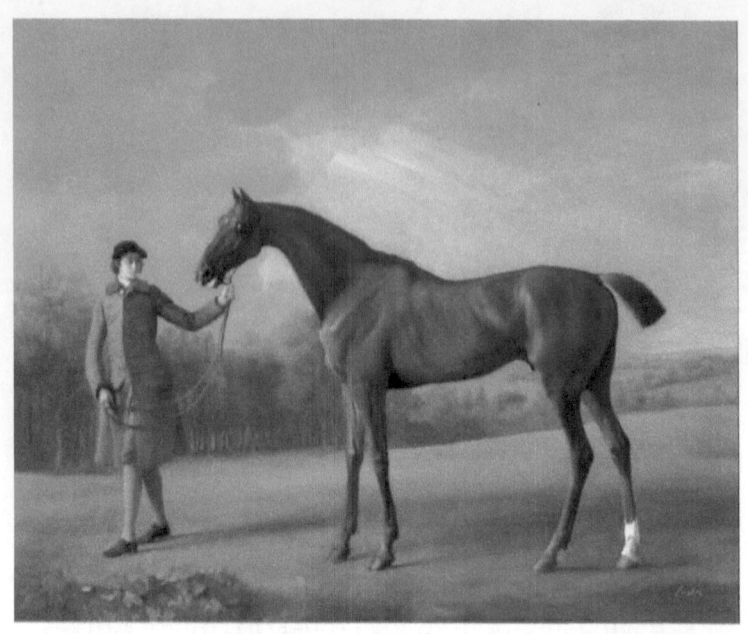

Lustre, held by a Groom, 1762, oil

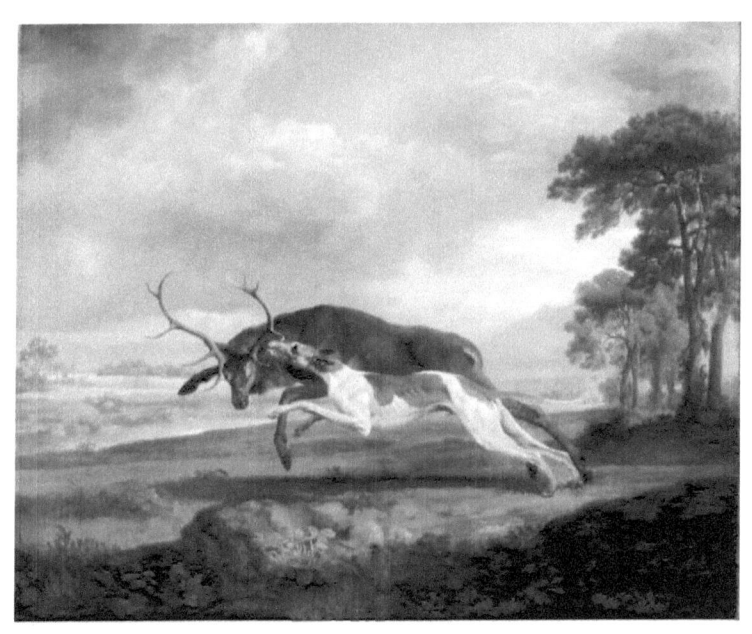

Hound Coursing a Stag, 1762, oil

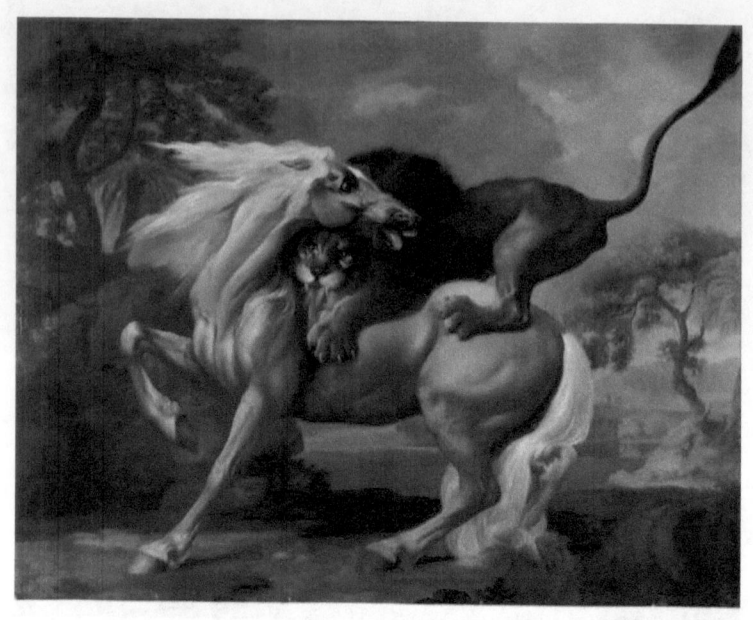

Horse Attacked by a Lion, c.1762, oil on canvas

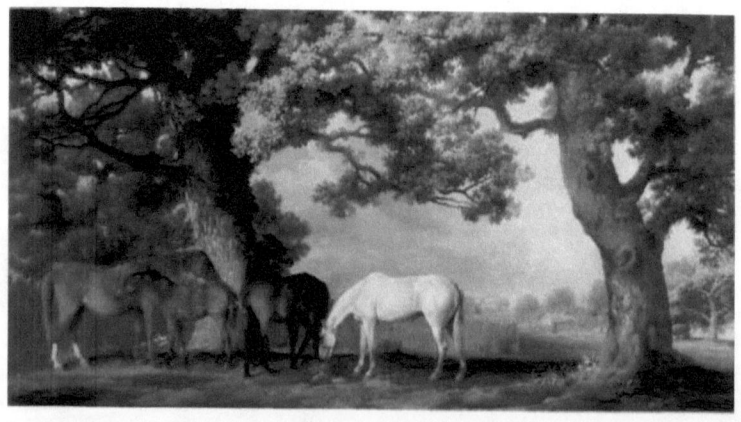

Mares and Foals in a Wooded Landscape, 1760-1762, oil on canvas

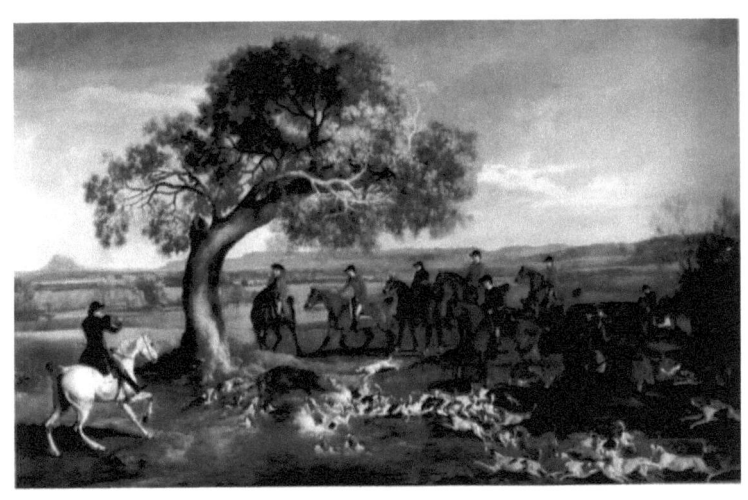

The Grosvenor Hunt, 1762, oil on canvas

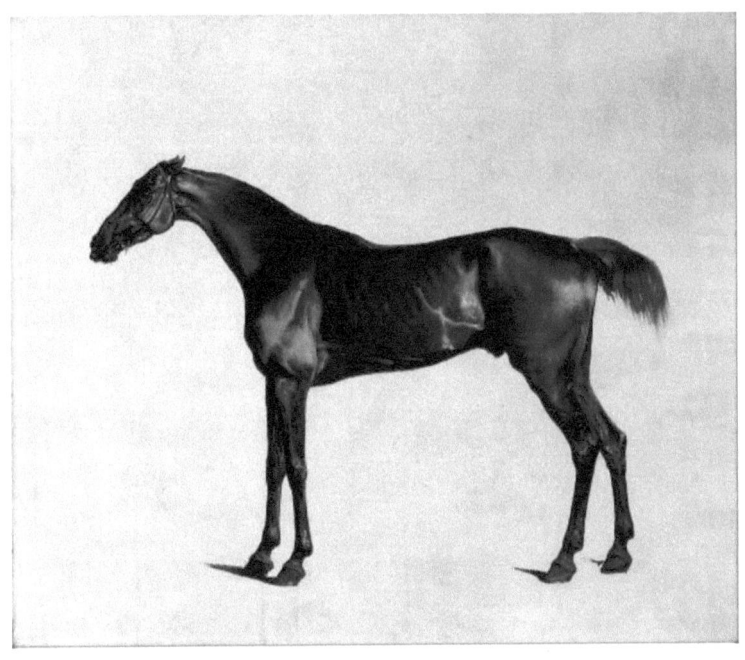

Pangloss, 1762, oil

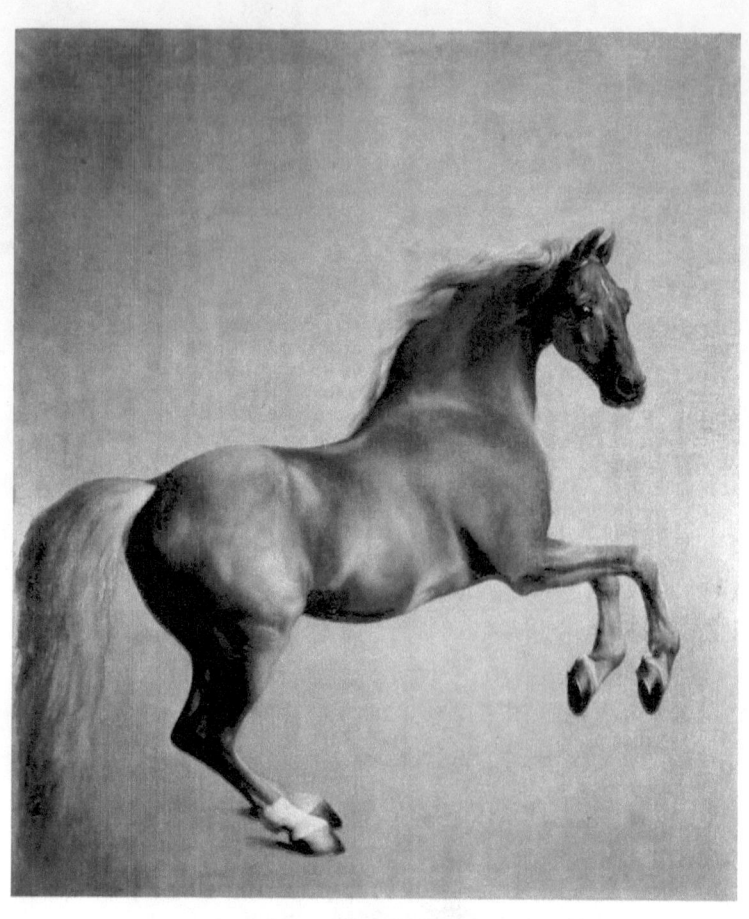

Whistlejacket, 1762, oil on canvas

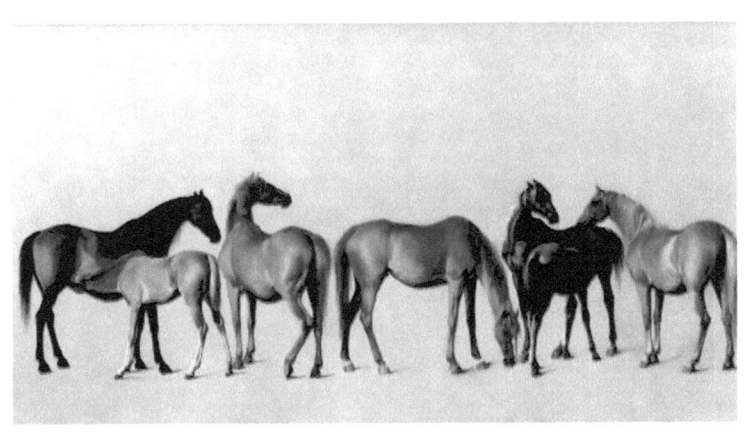

Mares and Foals, 1762, oil

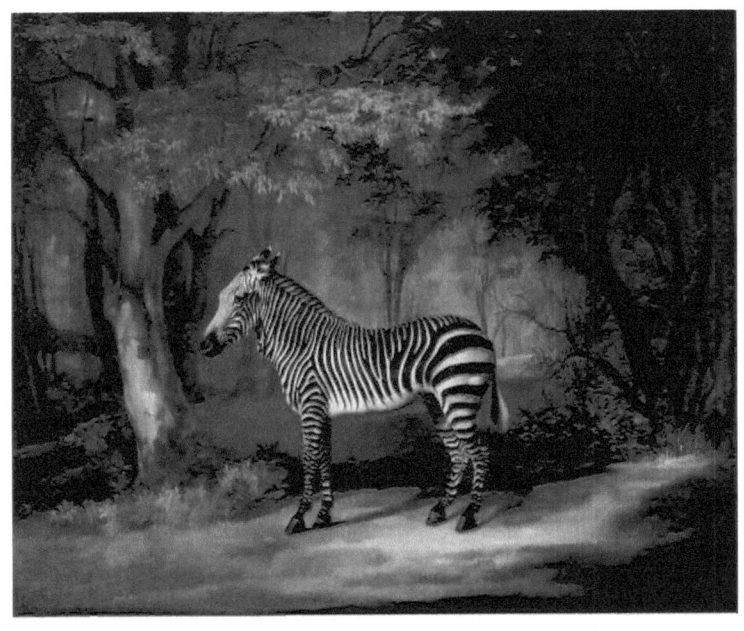

Zebra, 1763, oil

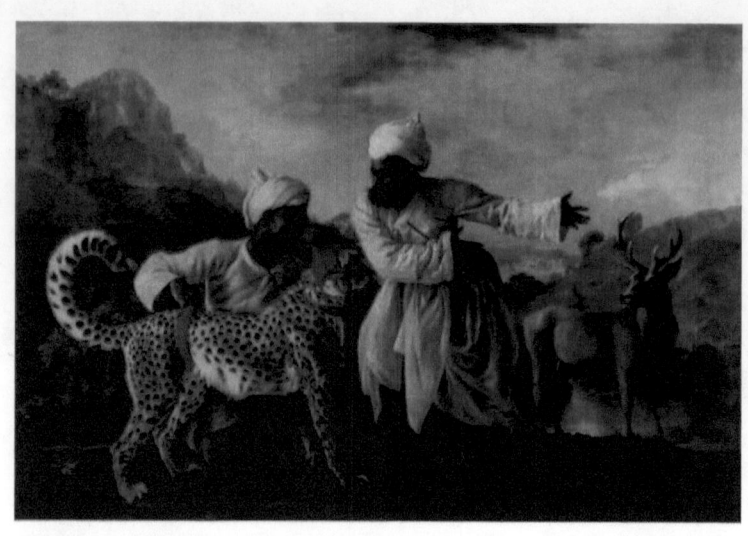

Cheetah with two Indian servants and a deer, 1765, oil on canvas

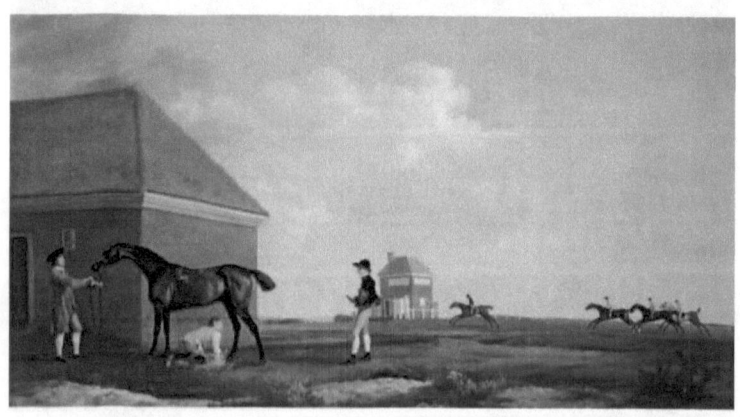

Gimcrack on Newmarket Heath, with a Trainer, a Stable lad, and a Jockey, 1765, oil on canvas

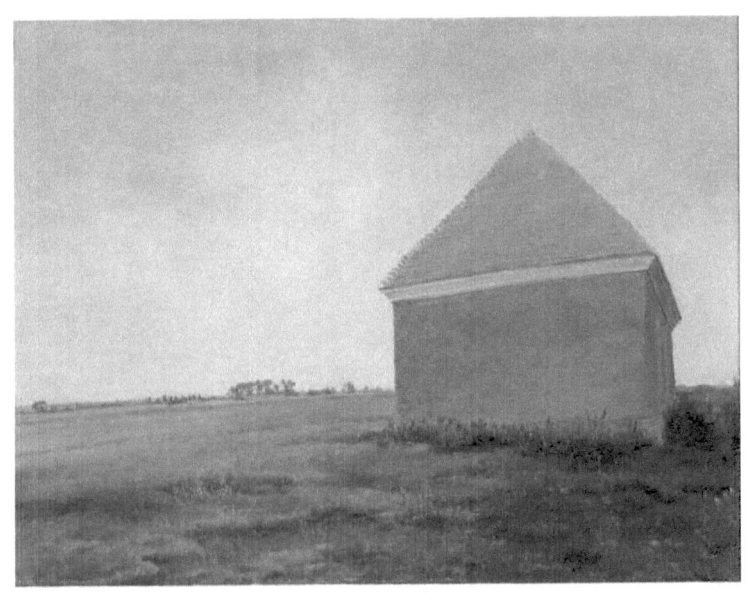

Newmarket Heath, with a Rubbing-down House, 1765,
oil on canvas

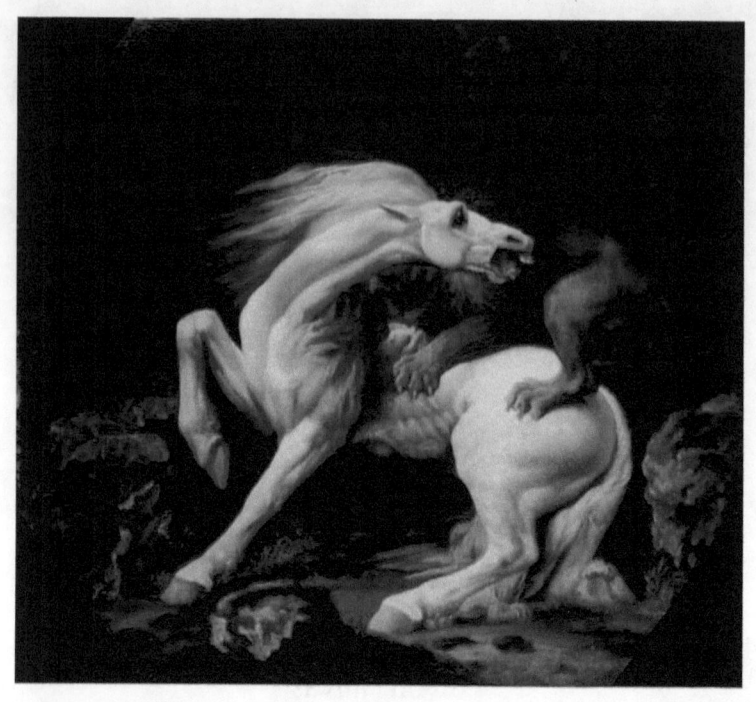

Horse Attacked by a Lion, 1762-1765, oil on canvas

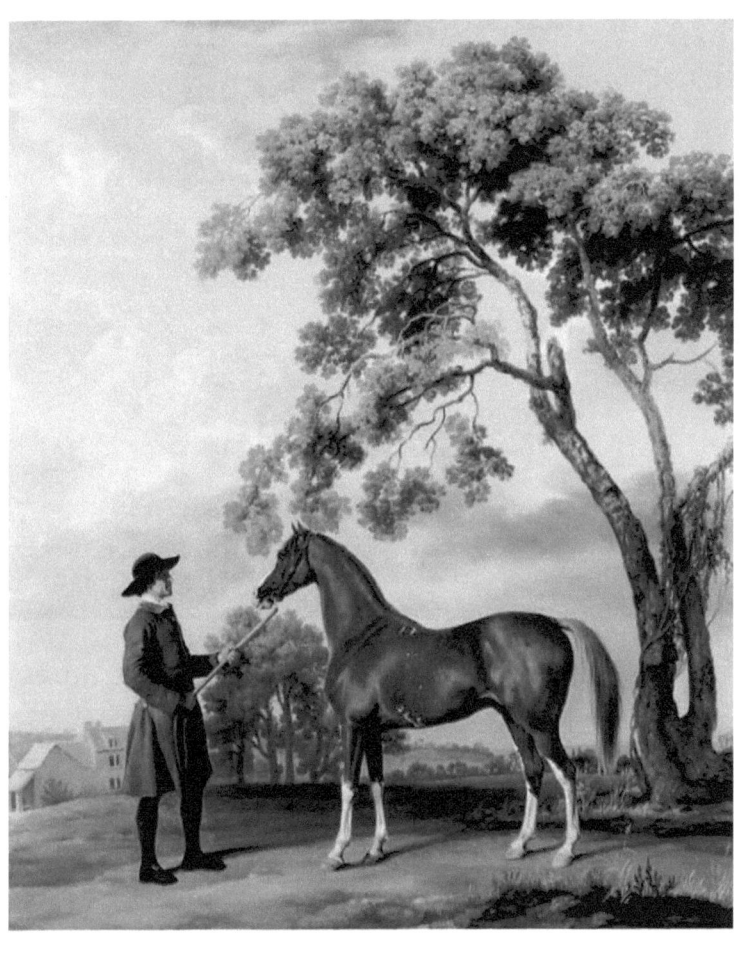

Lord Grosvenor's Arabian Stallion with a Groom,
c.1765, oil on canvas

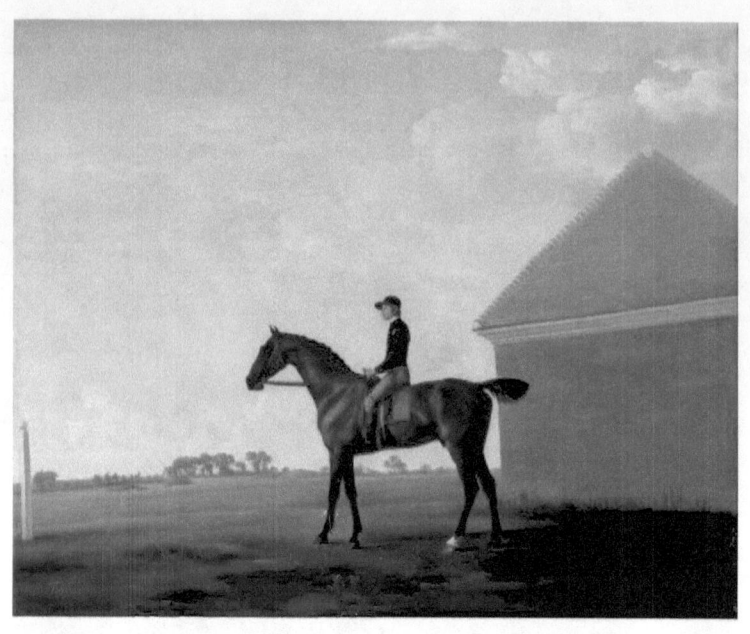

Turf, with Jockey up, at Newmarket, 1765, oil

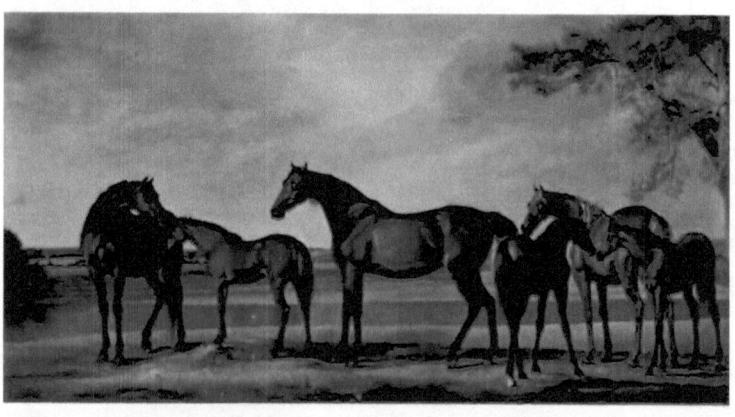

Mares and foals are anxious before a looming storm,
1764-1765, oil on canvas

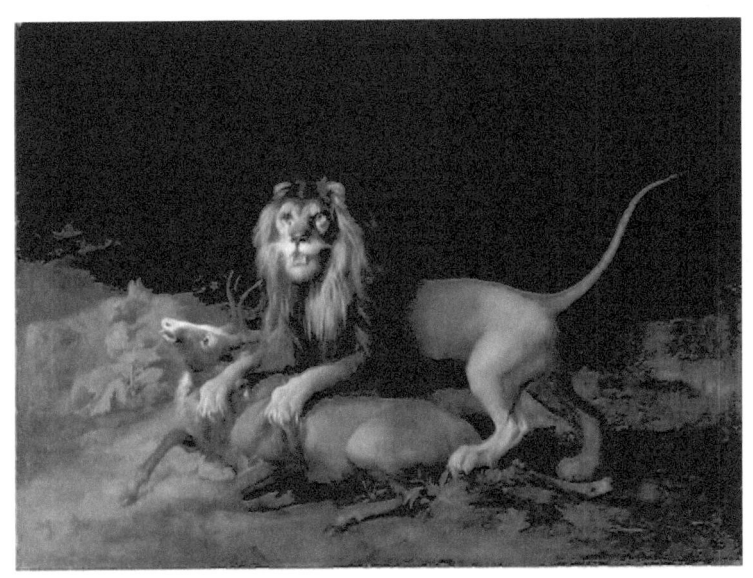

A Lion Attacking a Stag, 1765-1766, oil

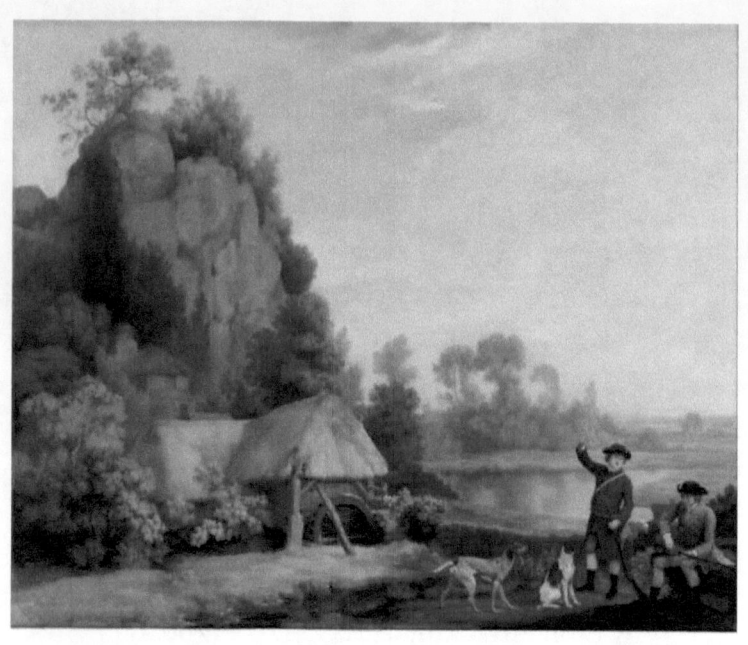

Two Gentlemen Going a Shooting, with a View of
Creswell Crags, Taken on the Spot, 1767, oil

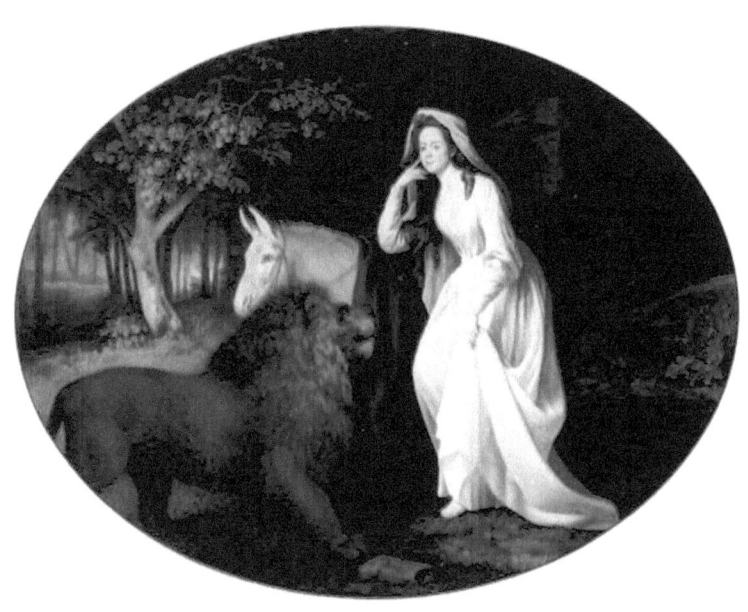

Portrait of Isabella Saltonstall, 1765-75, oil

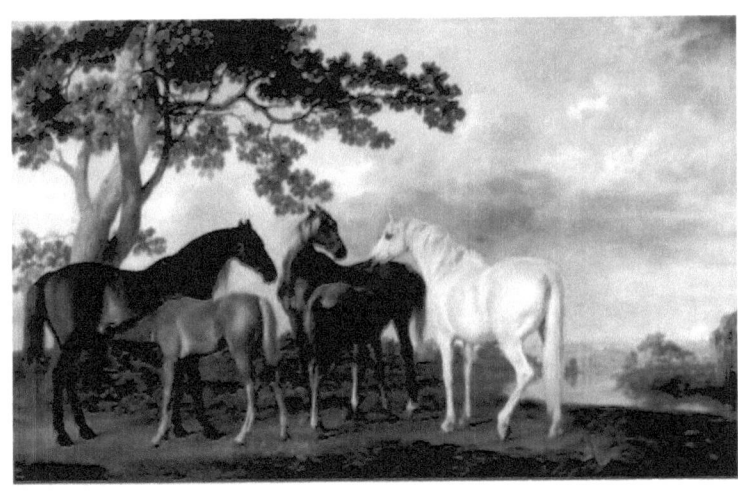

Mares and Foals in a River Landscape, 1763-1768, oil on canvas

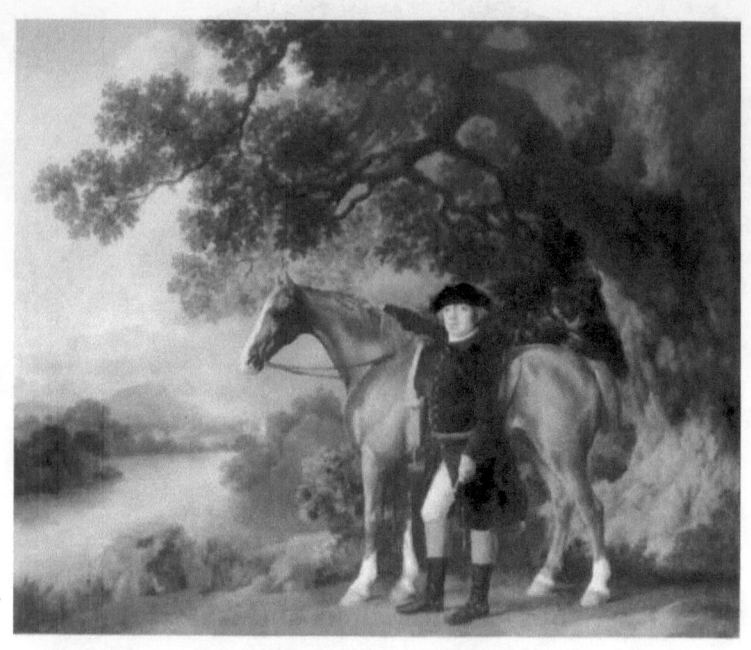

Portrait of a Huntsman, 1768, oil on canvas

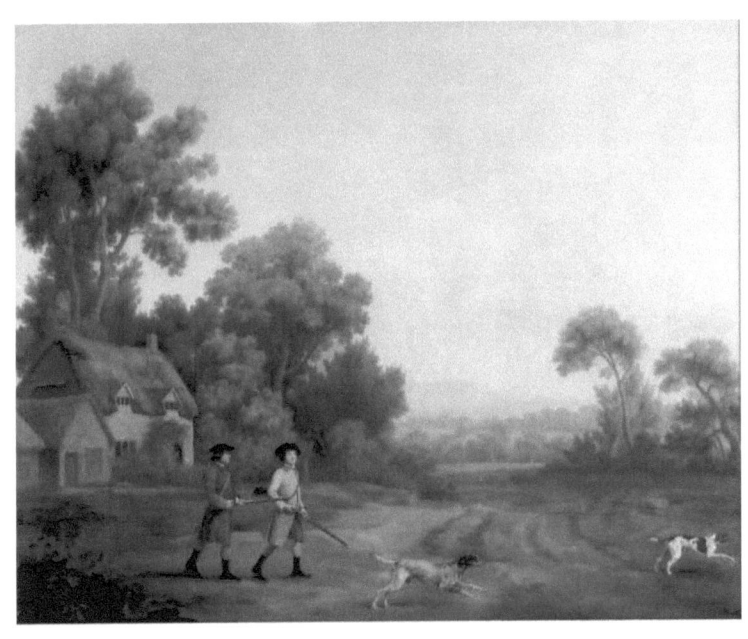

Two Gentlemen Going a Shooting, 1768, oil

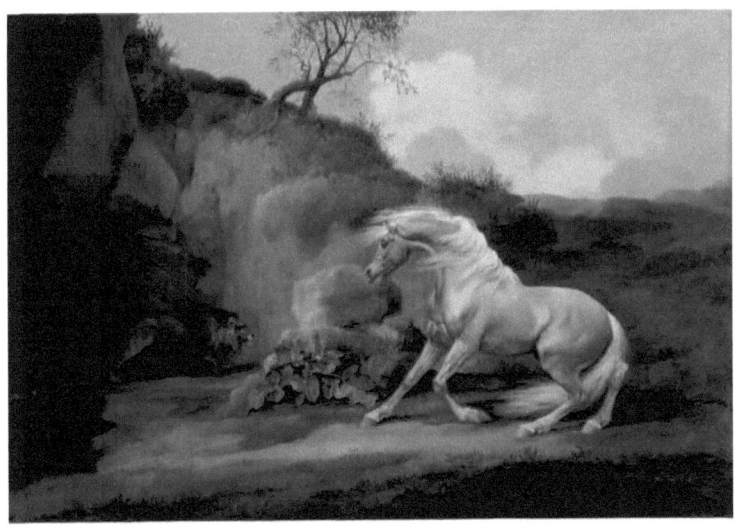

Horse Frightened by a Lion, 1762-1768, oil

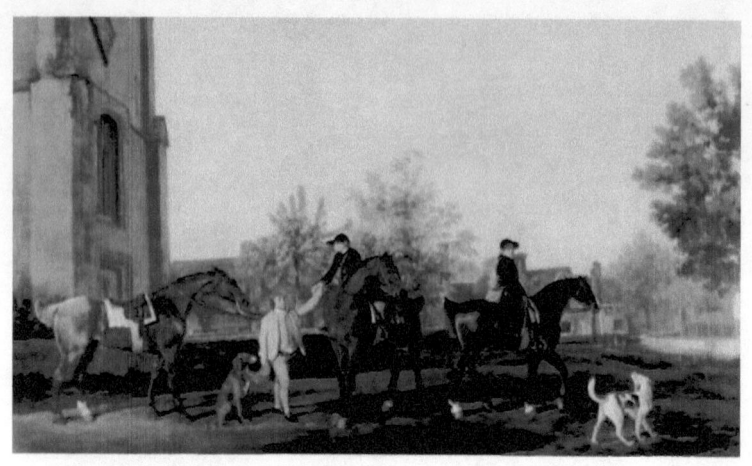

The Hunters leave Southill, 1763-1768, oil on canvas

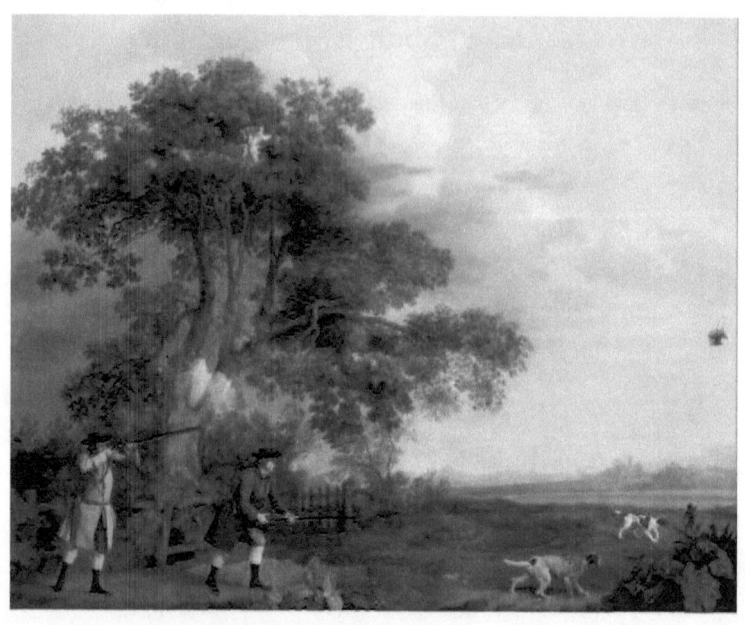

Two Gentlemen Shooting, 1769, oil

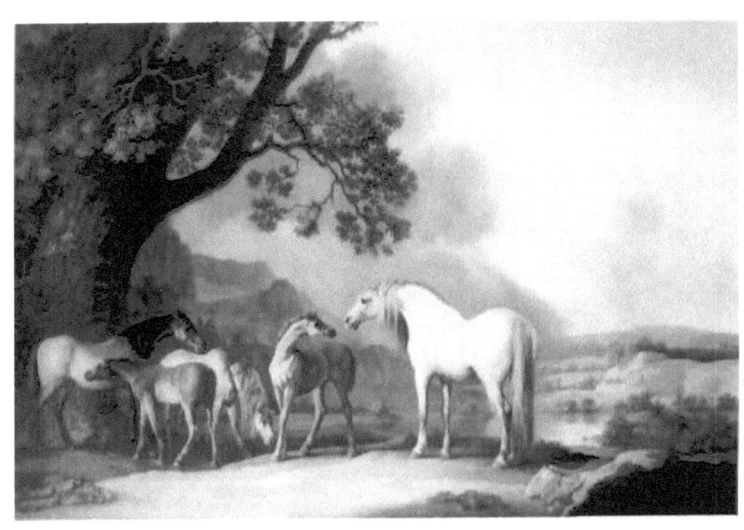

Mares and Foals in a Mountainous Landscape, 1769, oil on canvas

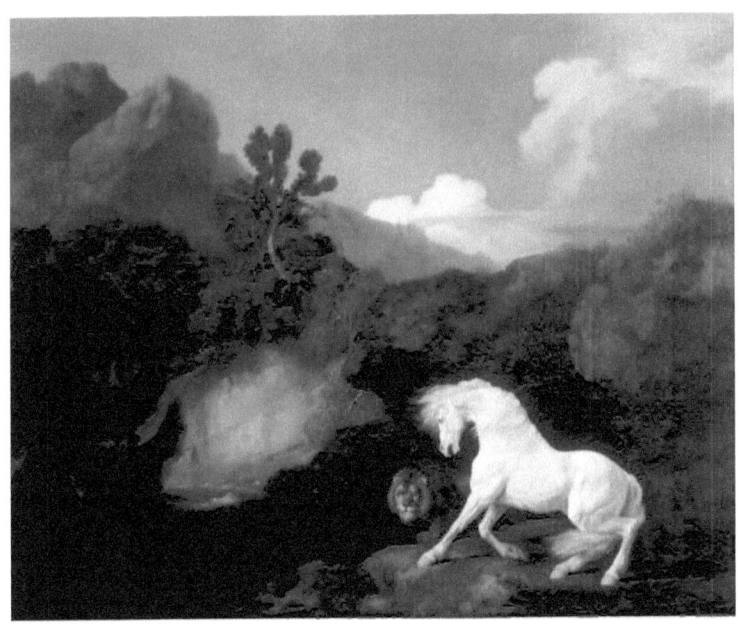

A Horse Frightened by a Lion, 1770, oil on canvas

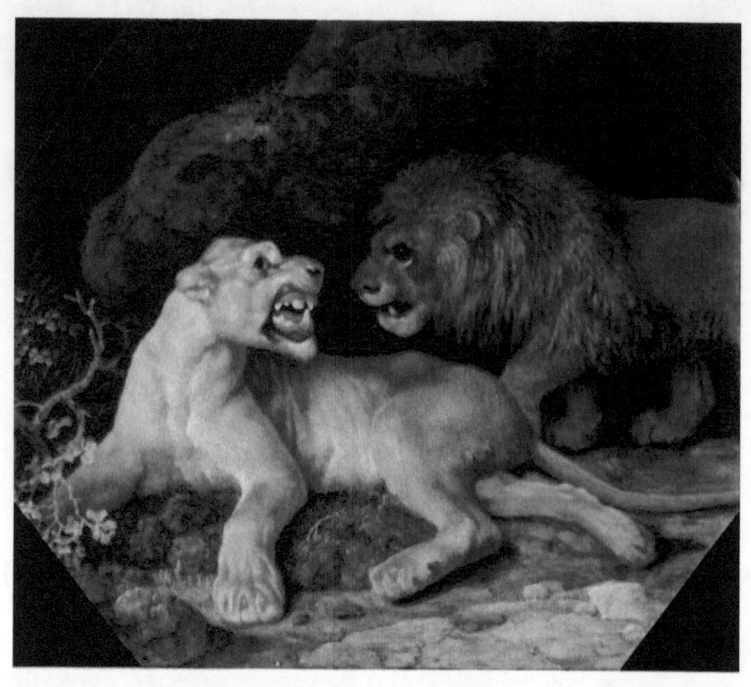

Lion and Lioness, 1770, Enamel on copper

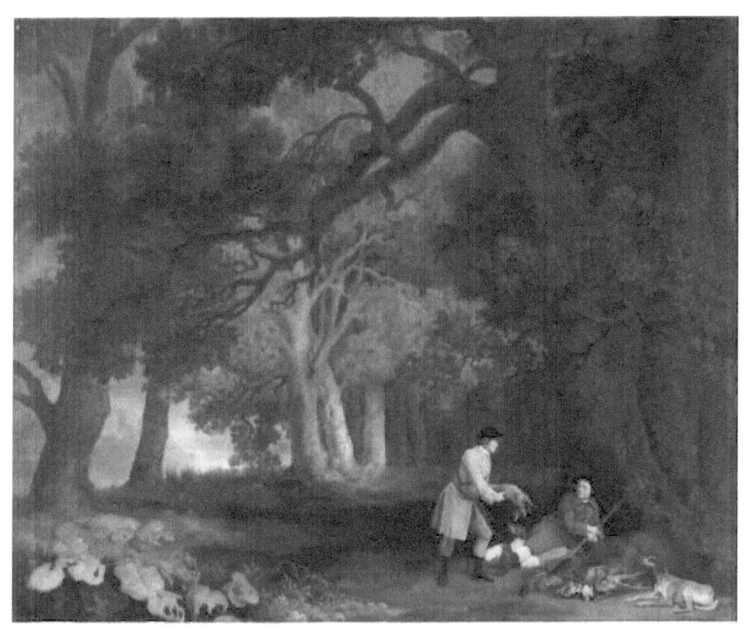

A Repose after Shooting, 1770, oil on canvas

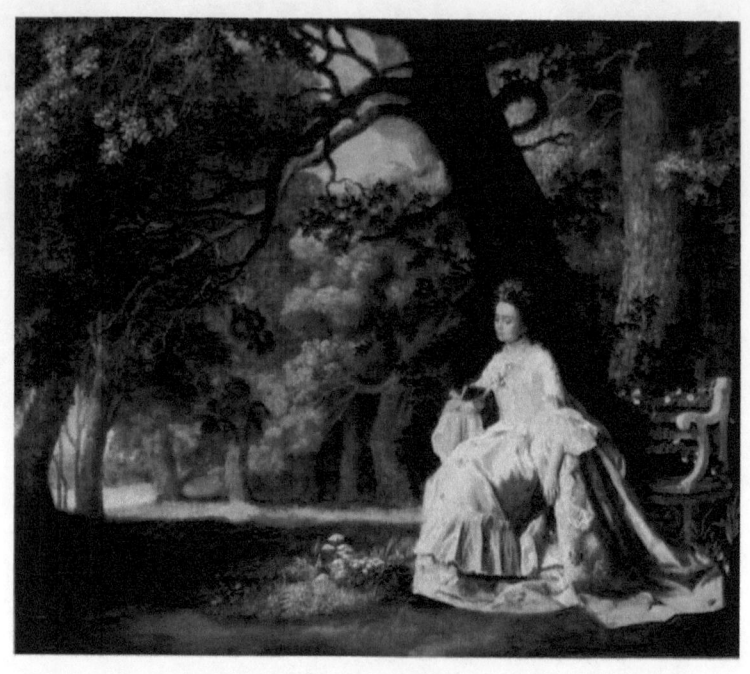

Lady Reading in a Wooded Park, 1768-1770, oil on canvas

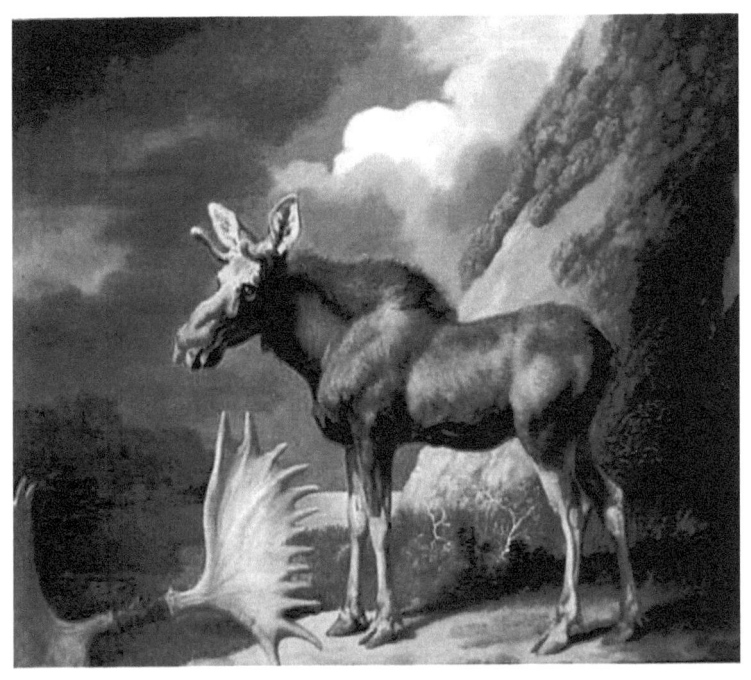

The Moose, 1773, oil on canvas

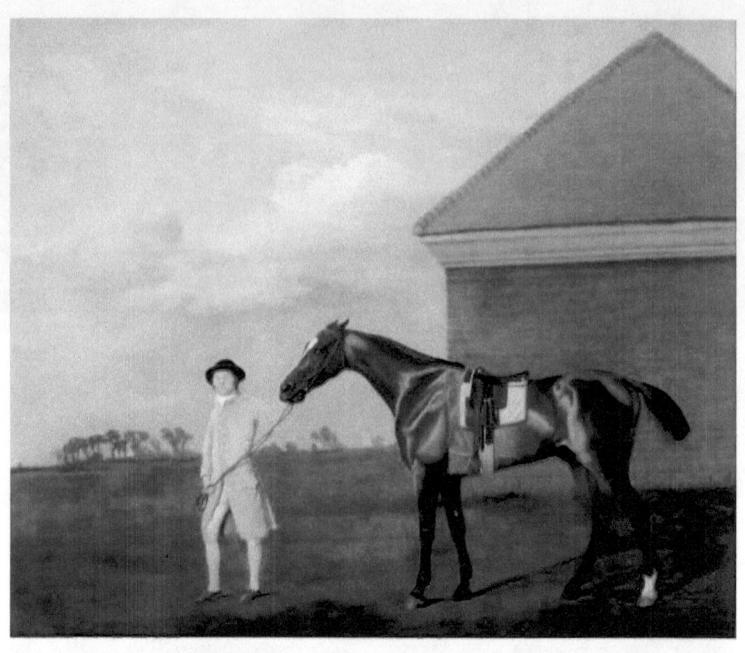

Firetail with his Trainer by the Rubbing-Down House
on Newmarket Heath, 1773, oil

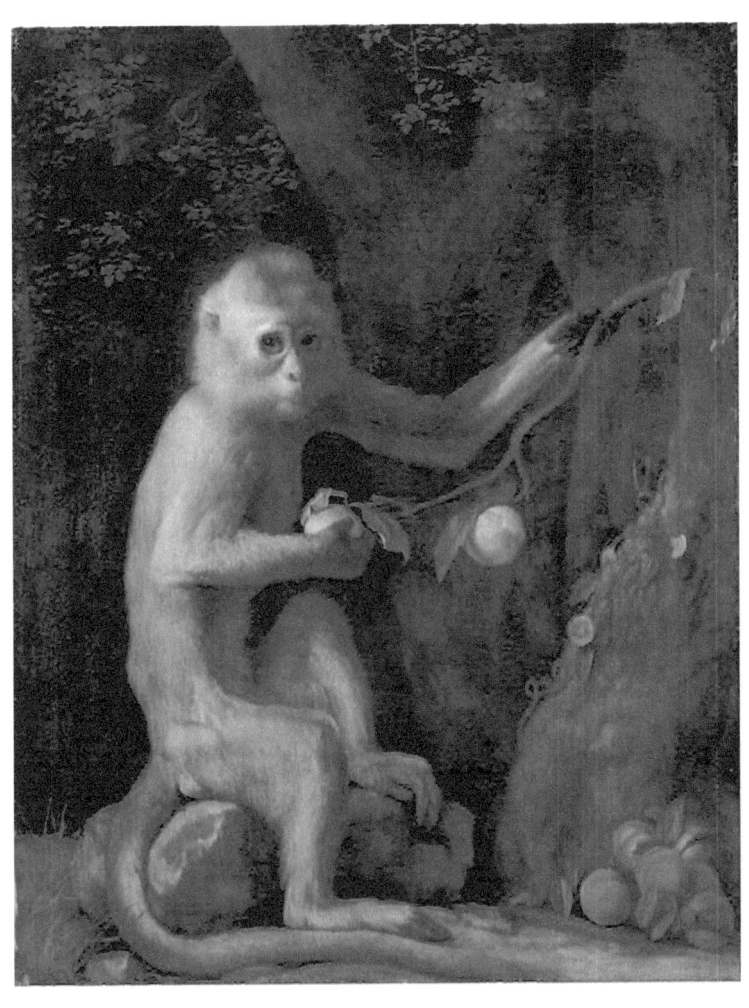

Portrait of a Monkey, 1774, oil on canvas

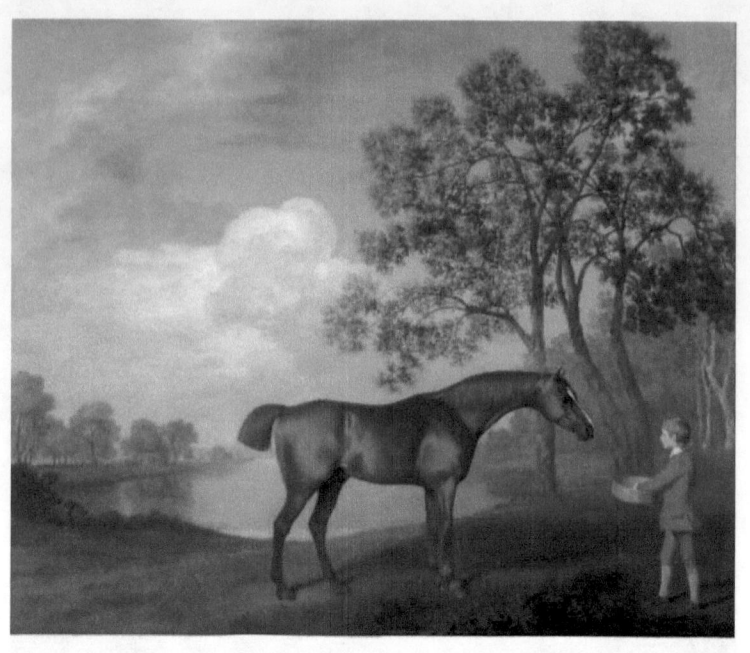

Pumpkin with a Stable Lad, 1774, oil on canvas

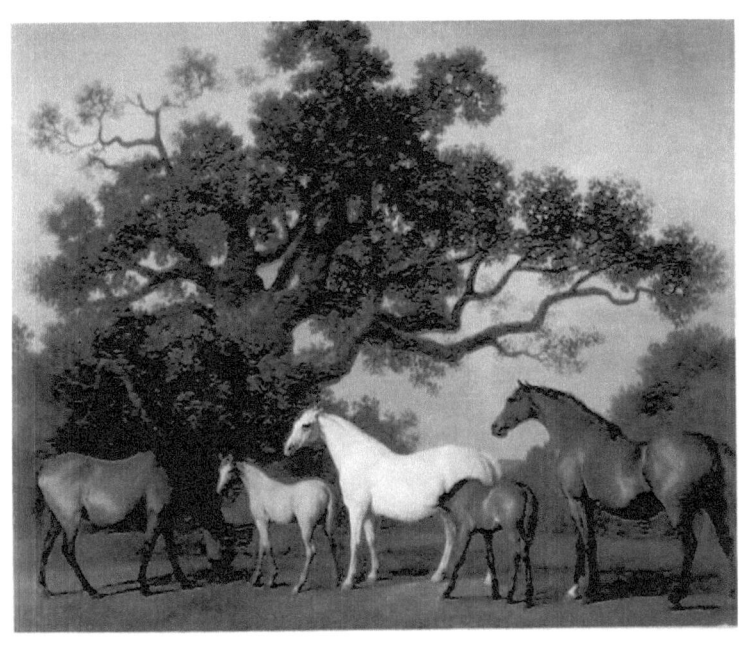

Mares and Foals under an Oak Tree, 1775, oil on canvas

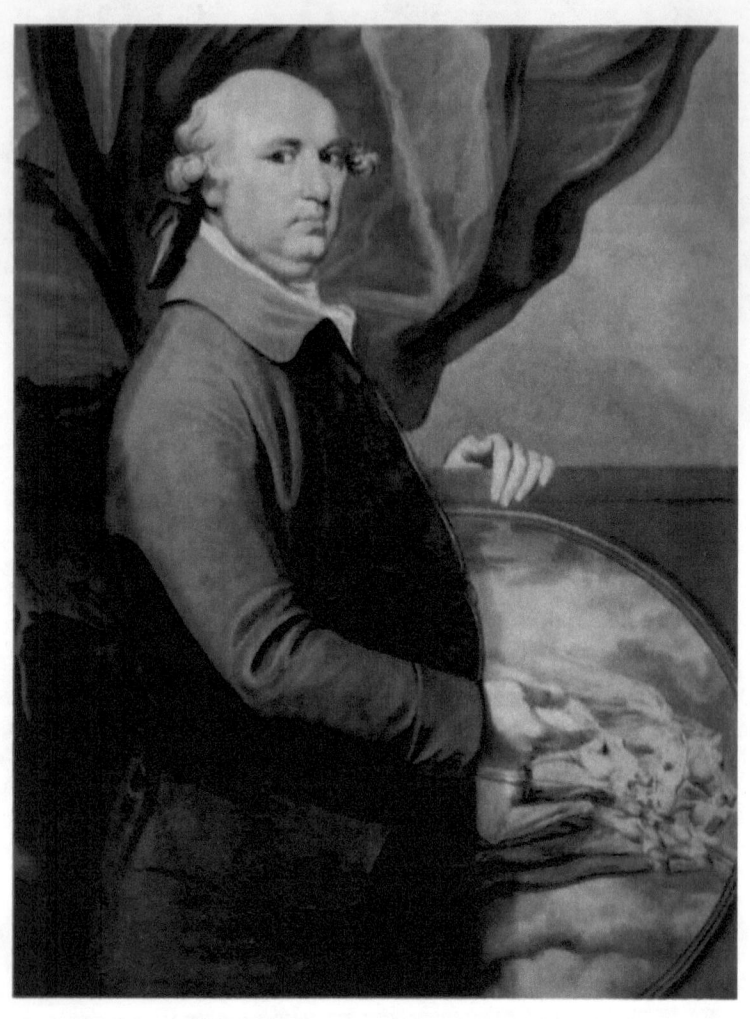

Self-Portrait, c.1765-c.1775, oil on wood

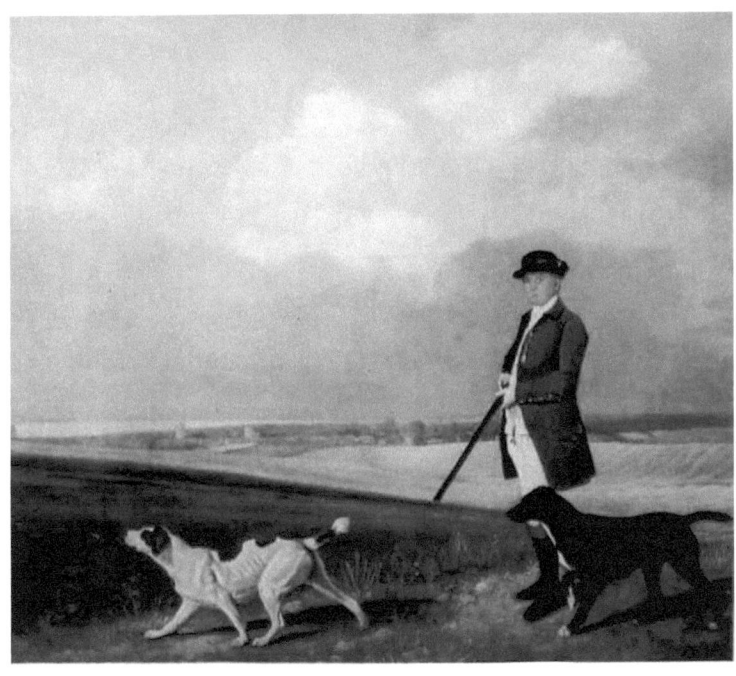

Sir John Nelthorpe, 6th Baronet out Shooting with his
Dogs in Barton Field, Lincolnshire, 1776, oil on panel

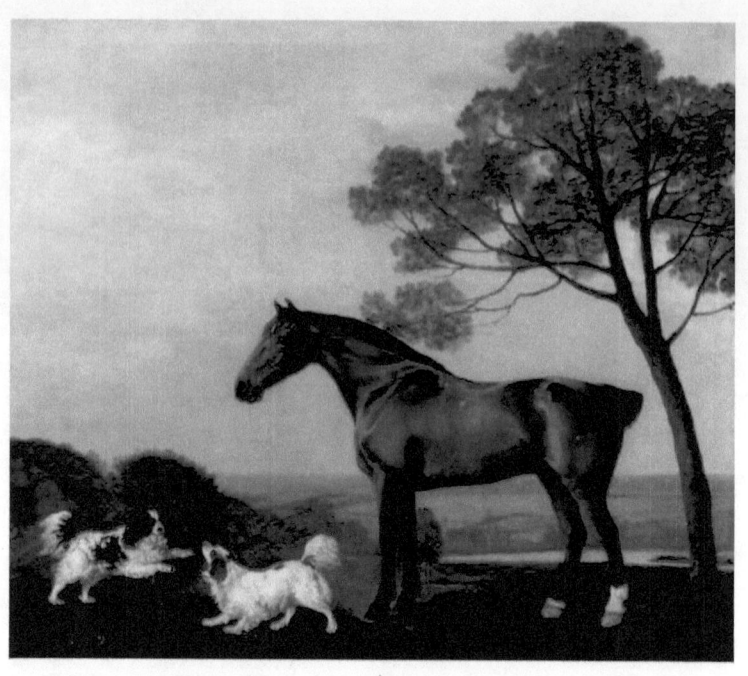

A Bay Hunter with Two Spaniels, 1777, oil on panel

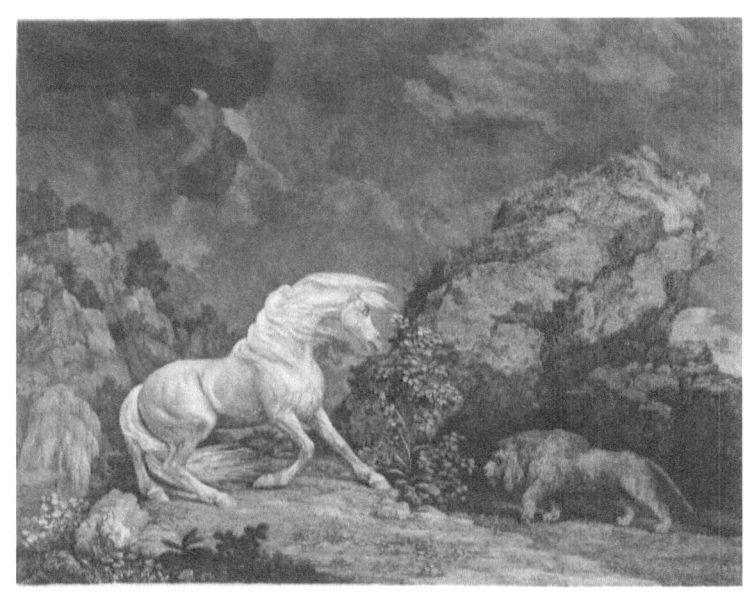

A Horse Affrighted by a Lion, 1777, etching

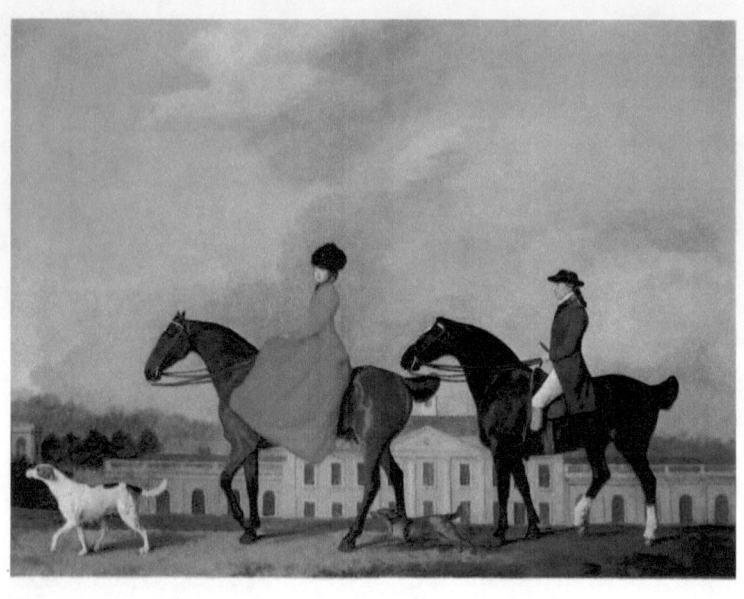

John and Sophia Musters riding at Colwick Hall, 1777,
oil on panel

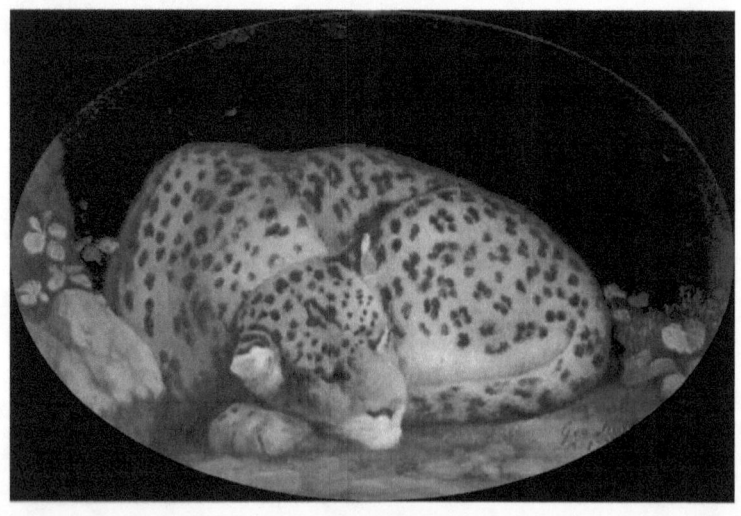

Sleeping Leopard, 1777, Enamel on Wedgwood biscuit
earthenware

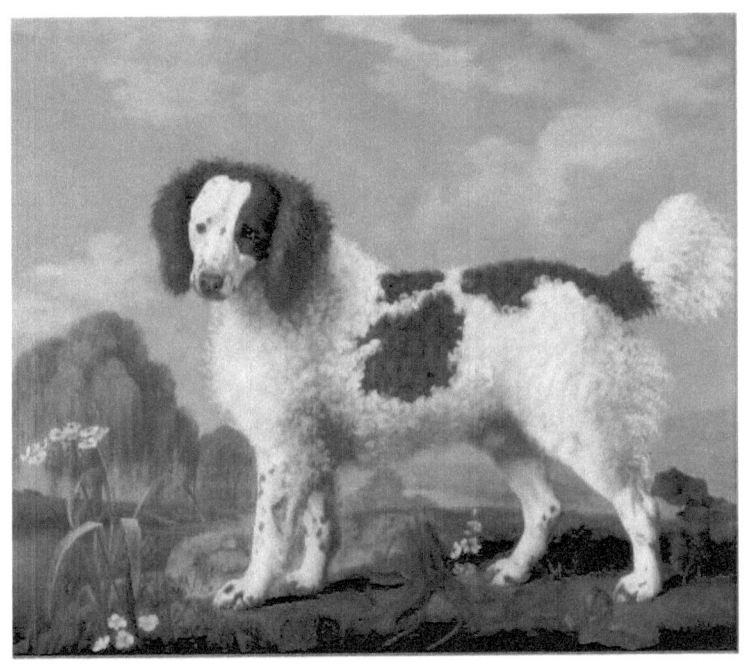

Brown and White Norfolk or Water Spaniel, 1778, oil

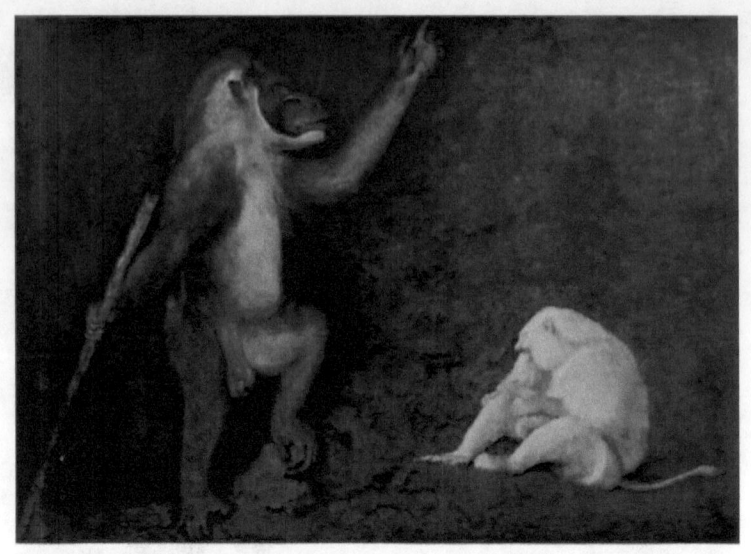

Pavian and Albino Makake, c.1780, oil on canvas

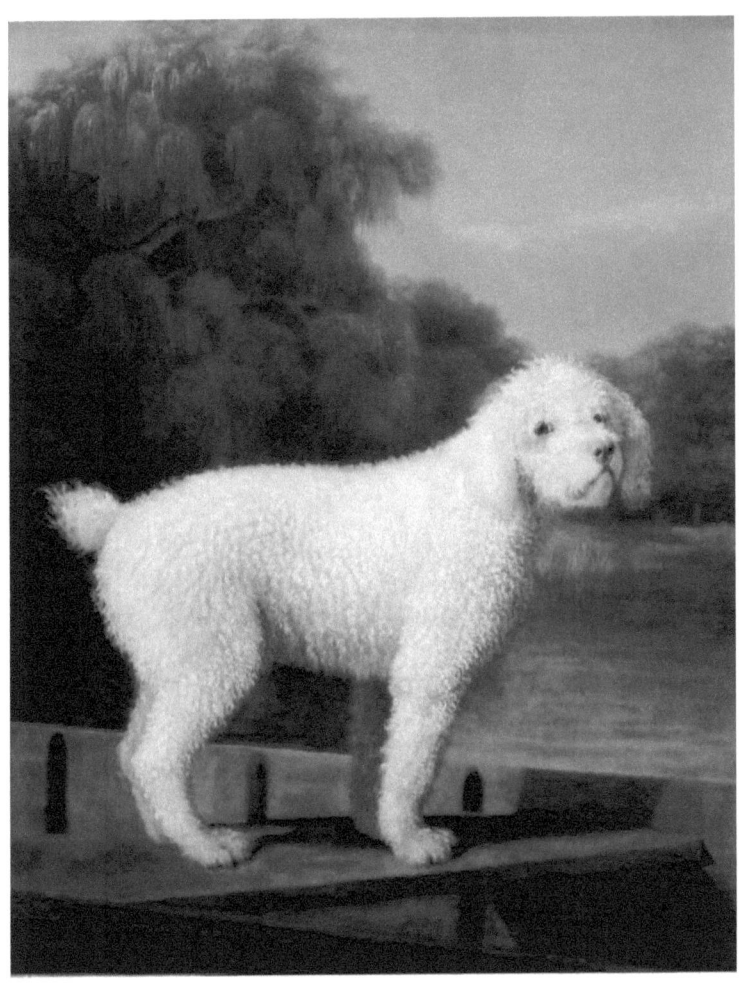

White Poodle in a Punt, 1780, oil

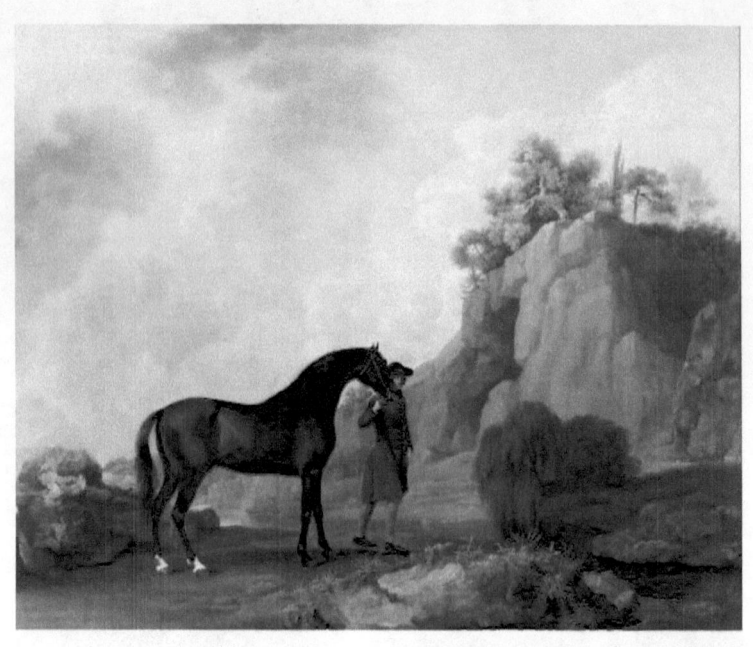

The Marquess of Rockingham's Arabian Stallion (led by a Groom at Creswell Crags), 1780, oil

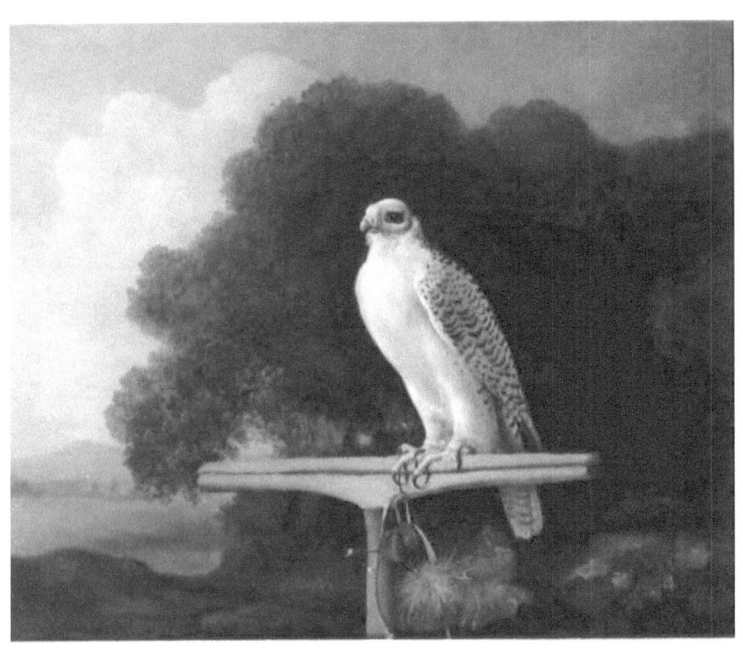

Greenland Falcon, 1780, oil

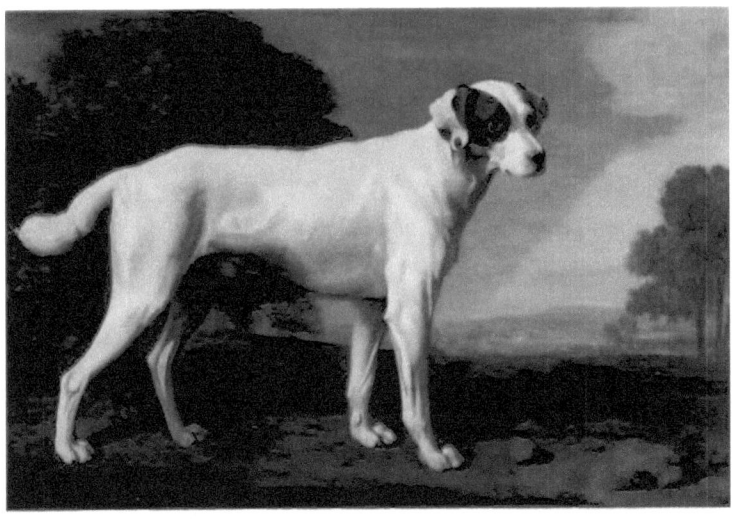

Viscount Gormanston's White Dog, 1781, oil on canvas

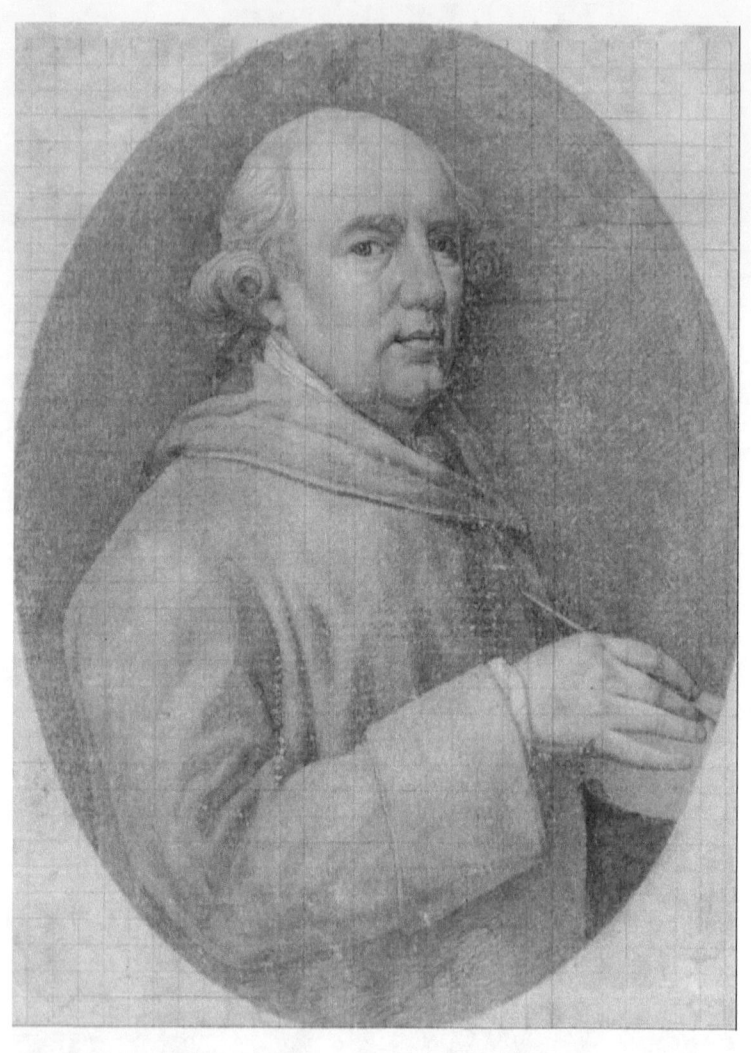

Study for the Self-portrait in Enamel, 1781, drawing

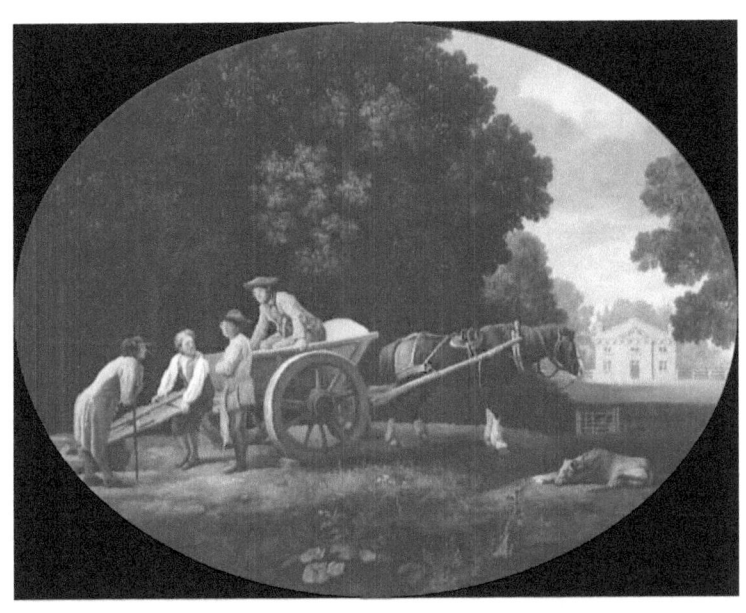

Labourers, 1781, oil on canvas

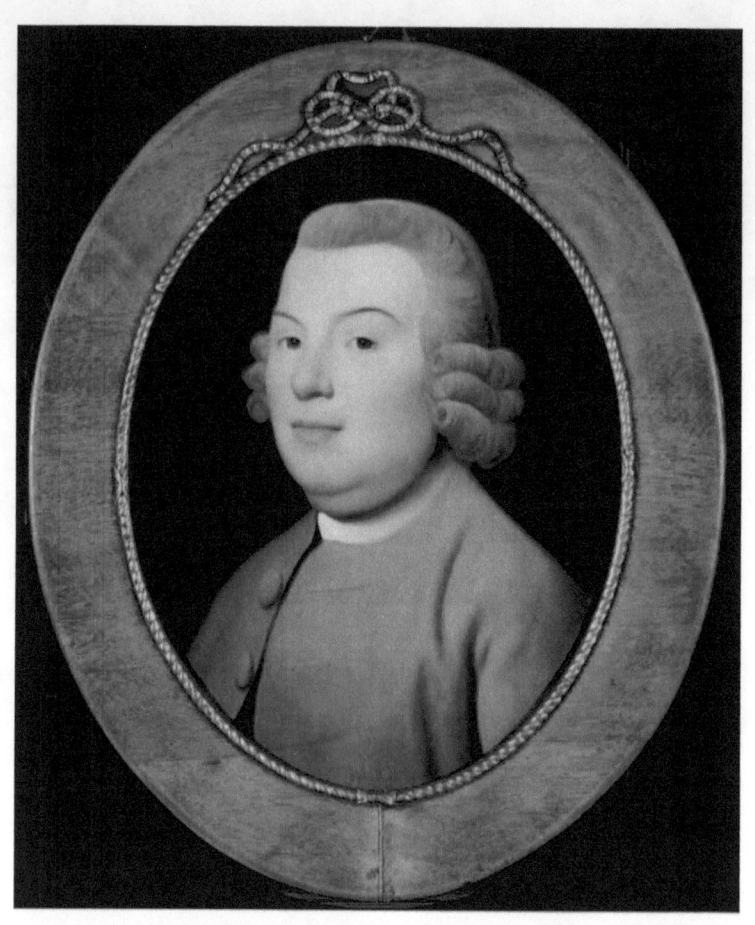

Mr. Hospey Walker, 1783, oil

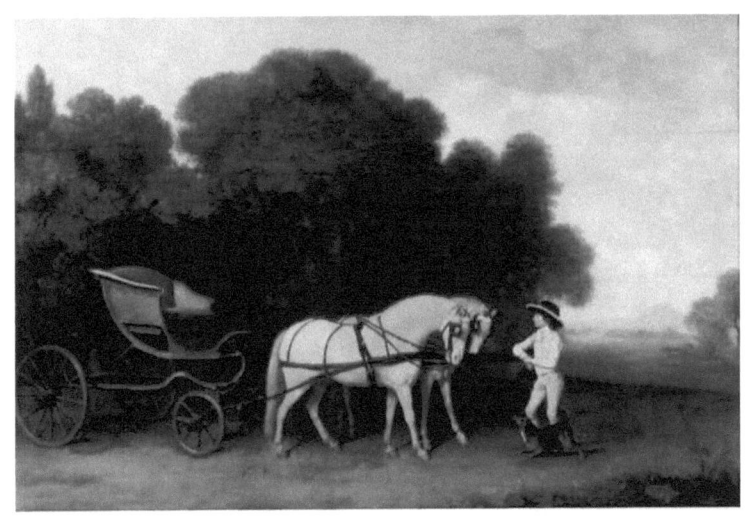

Phaeton with a Pair of Cream Ponies and a Stable-Lad, 1784, oil

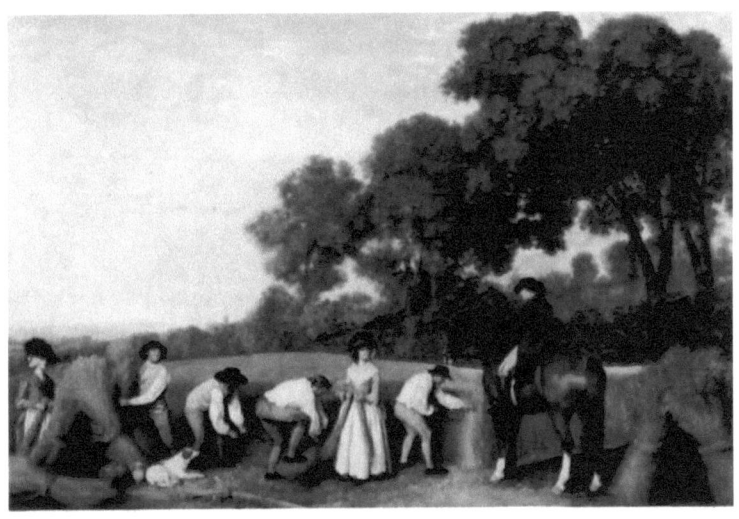

Harvest, 1785, oil on canvas

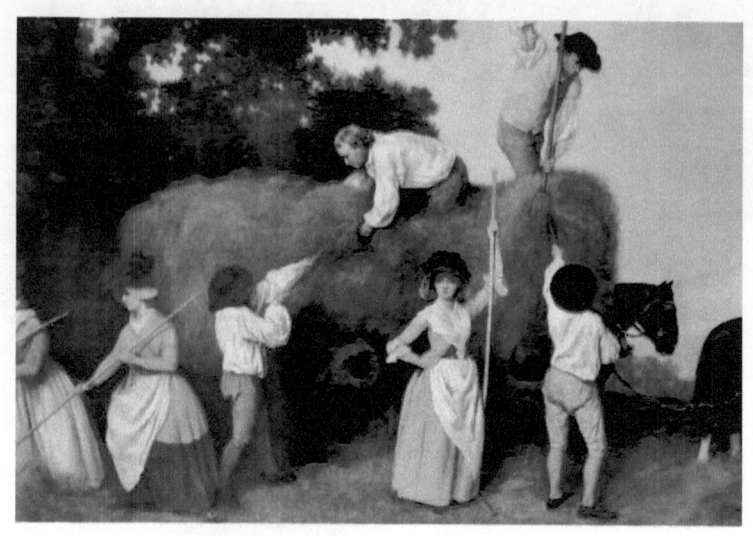

Haymakers, 1785, oil

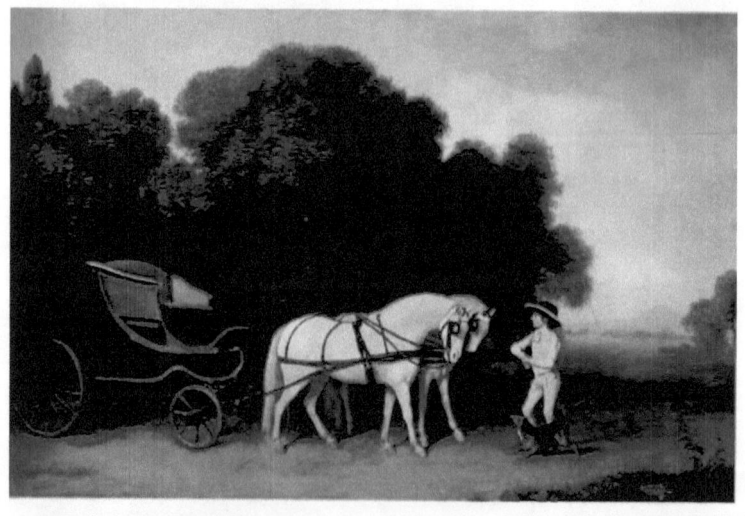

Park Phaeton with a Pair of Cream Pontes in Charge of
a Stable Lad with a Dog, 1780-1785, oil on canvas

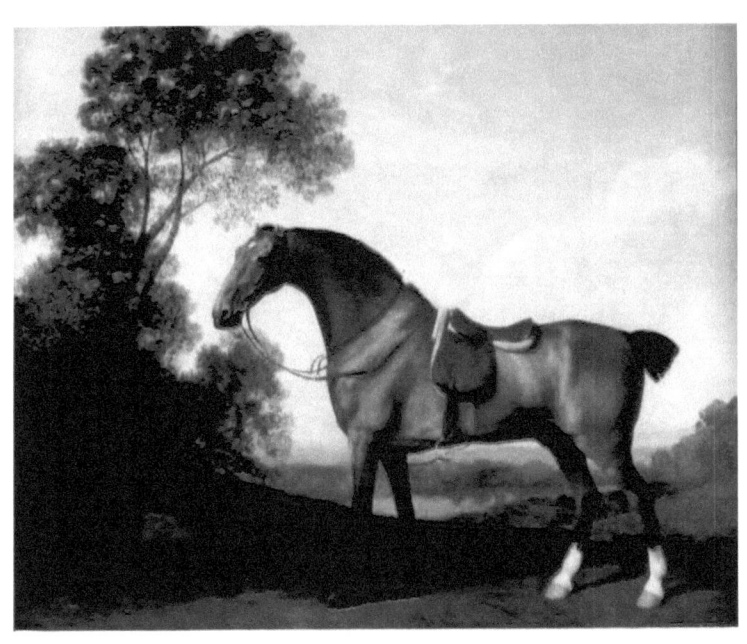

A Saddled Bay Hunter, 1786, oil on panel

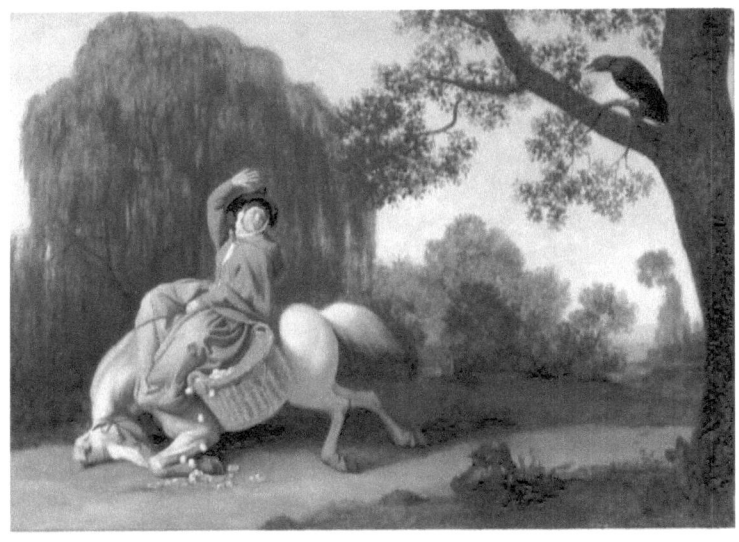

The Farmer's Wife and the Raven, 1786, iol

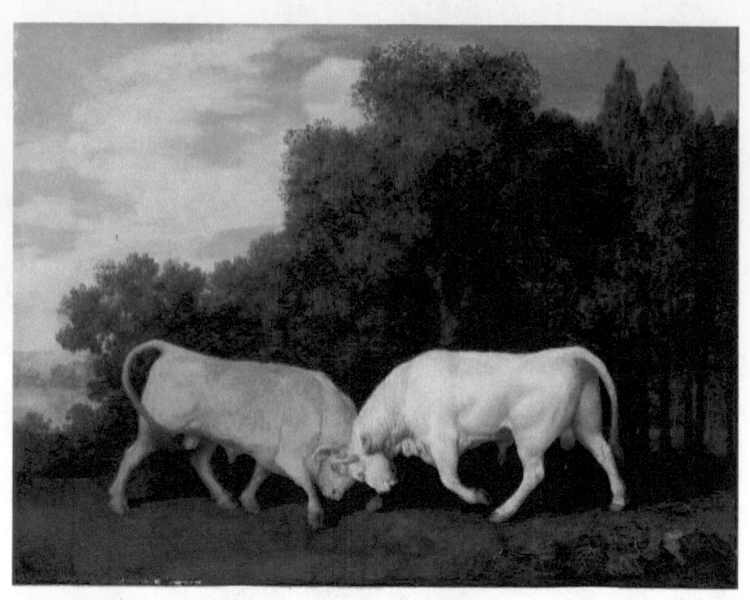

Bulls Fighting, 1786, oil

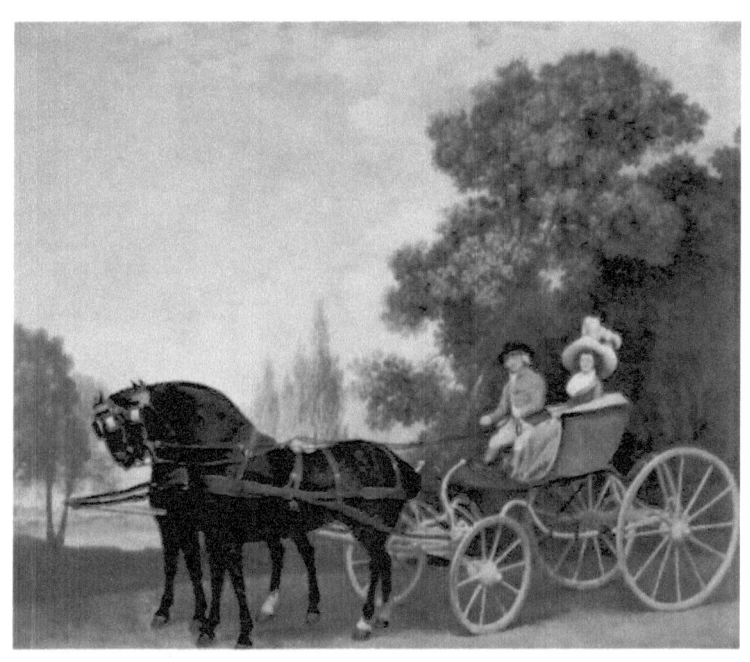

Lord and Lady in a Phaeton, 1787, oil on wood

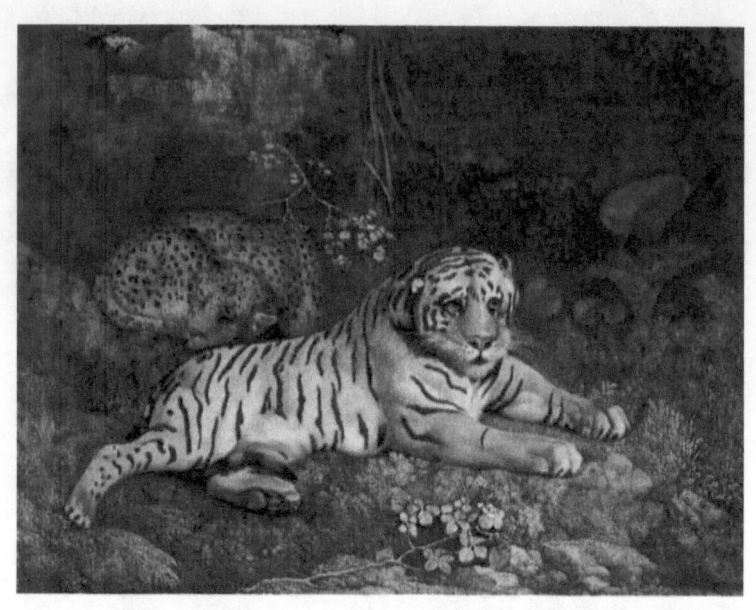

A Tiger and a Sleeping Leopard, 1788, etching

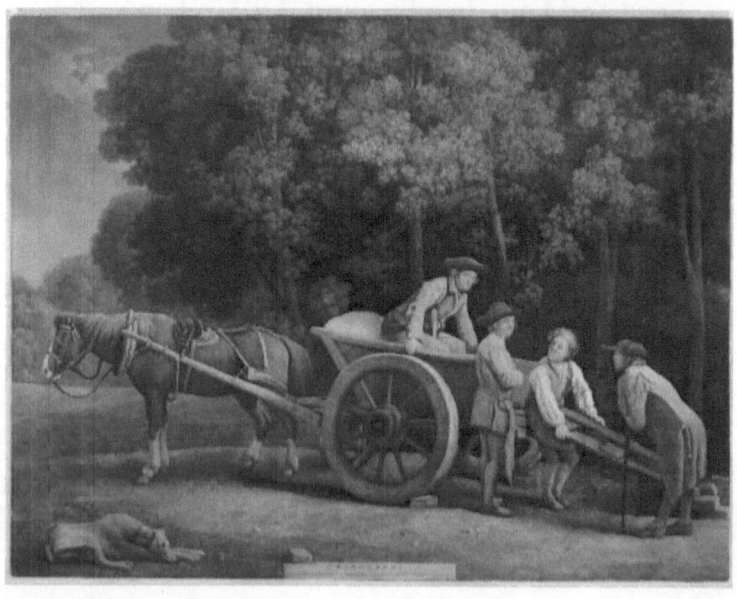

Labourers, 1789, etching

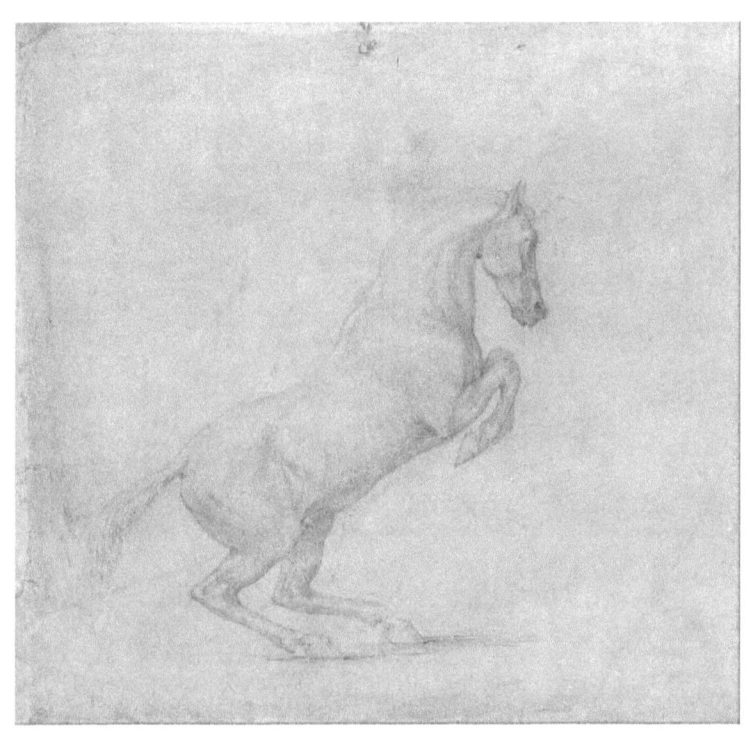

A Prancing Horse, Facing Right, 1790, drawing

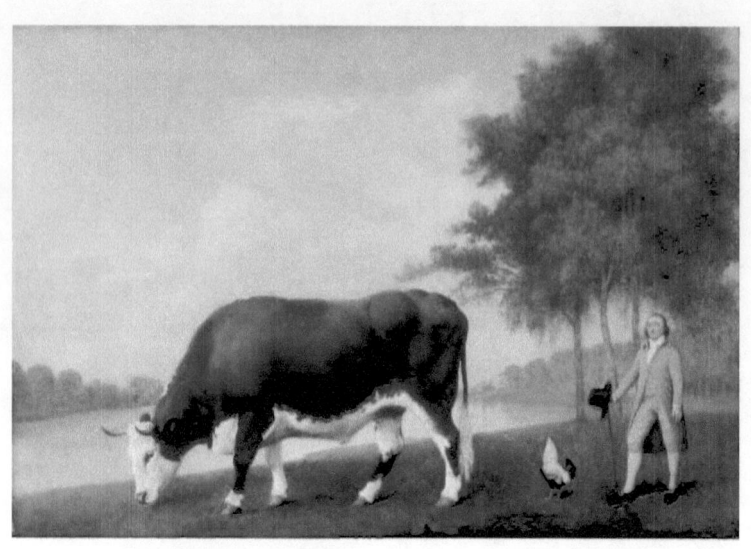

The Lincolnshire Ox, 1790, oil

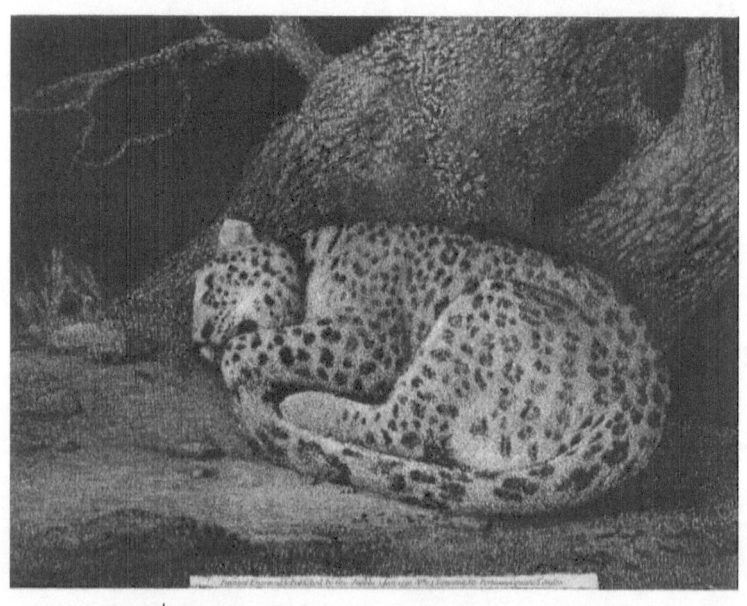

A Sleeping Leopard, 1791, etching

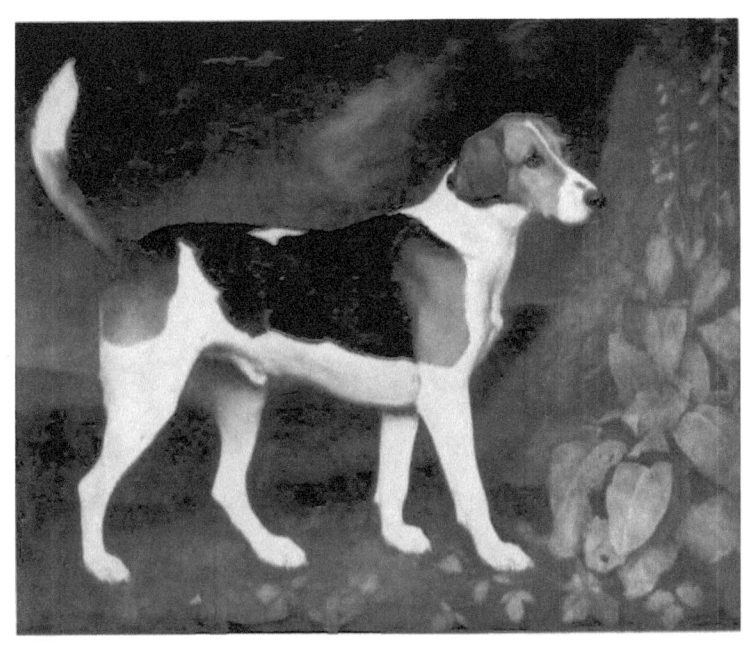

A Foxhound, Ringwod, 1792, oil on canvas

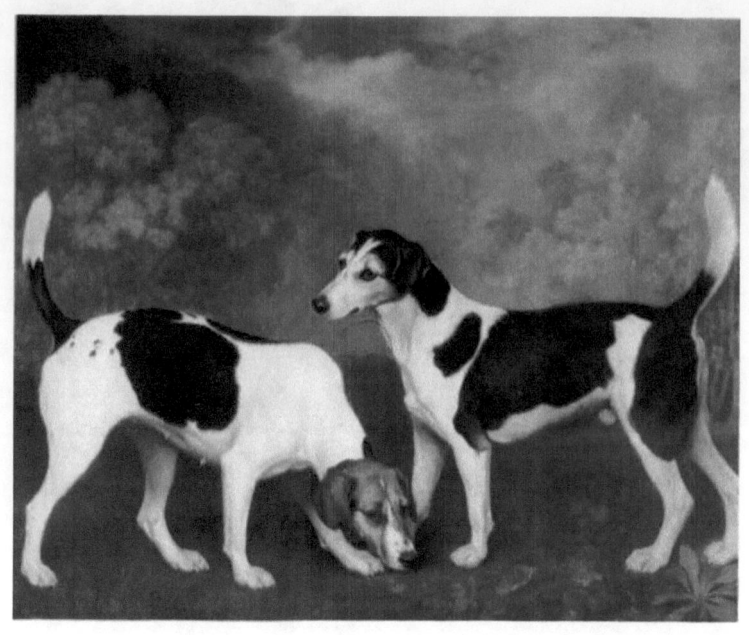

Hound and Bitch in a Landscape, 1792, oil on canvas

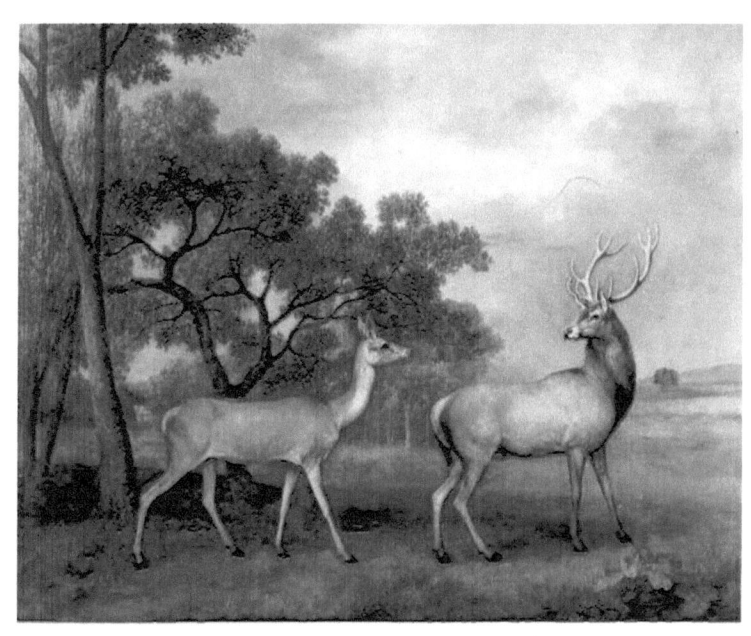

Red Deer Stag and Hind, 1792, oil on canvas

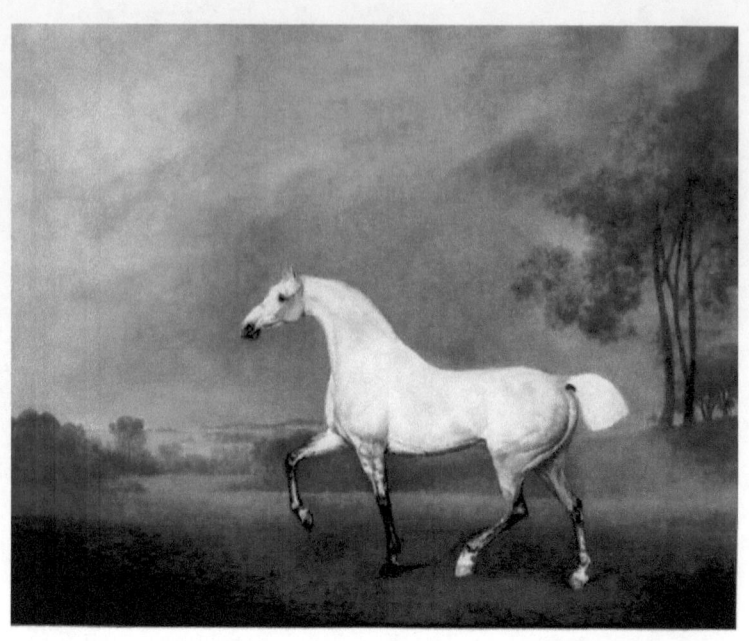

A Grey Horse, 1793, oil on canvas

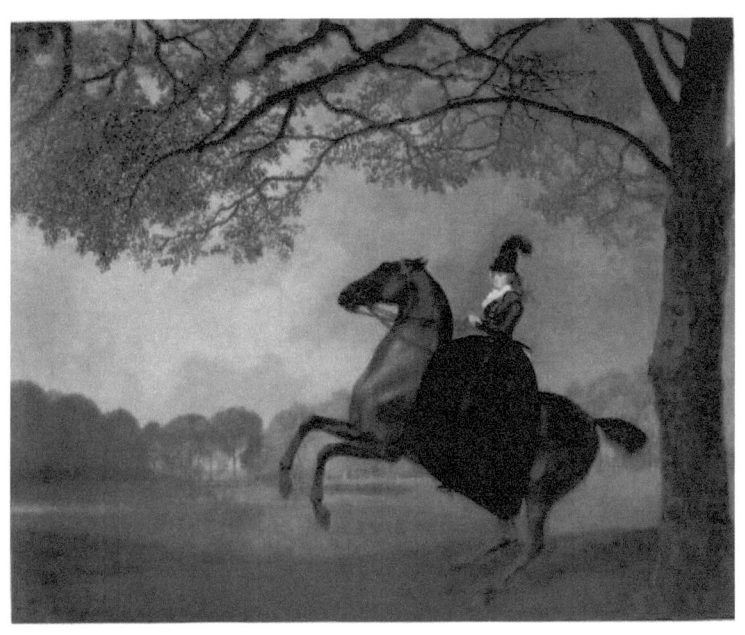

Laetitia, Lady Lade, 1793, oil on canvas

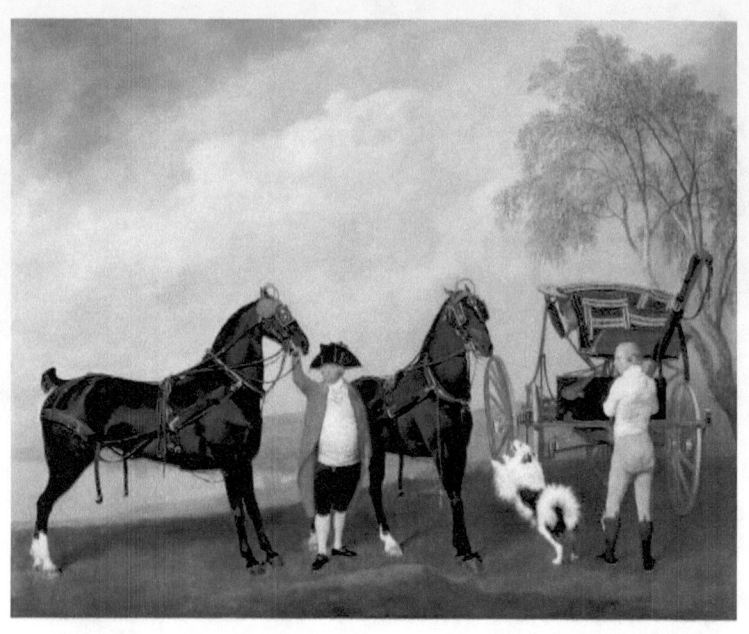

Prince of Wales Phaeton, 1793, oil on canvas

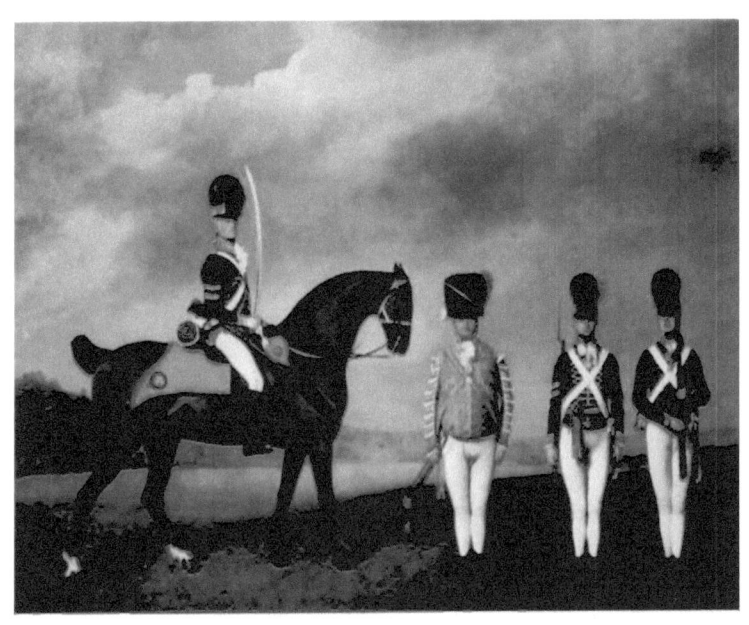

Soldiers of the 10th Dragoon Regiment, 1793, oil on canvas

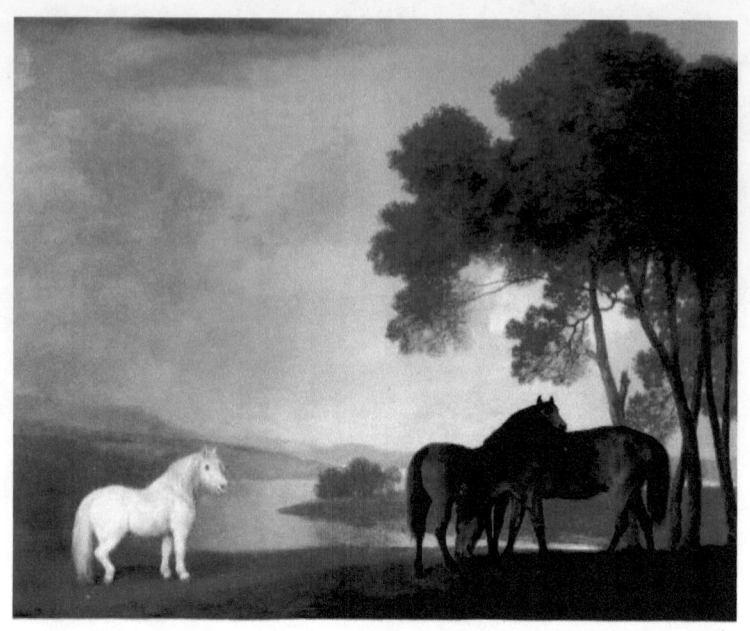

Two Bay Mares and a Grey Pony In a Landscape, 1793,
oil on canvas

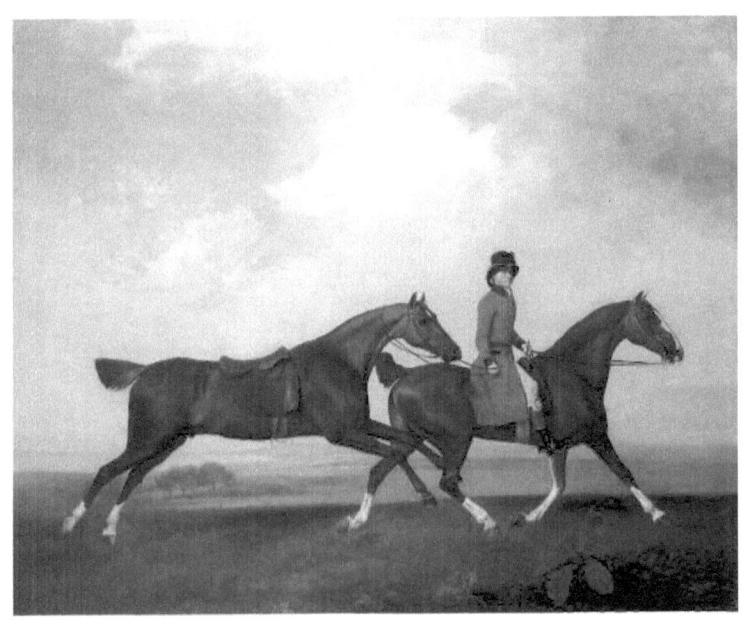

William Anderson with two saddle-horses, 1793, oil on canvas

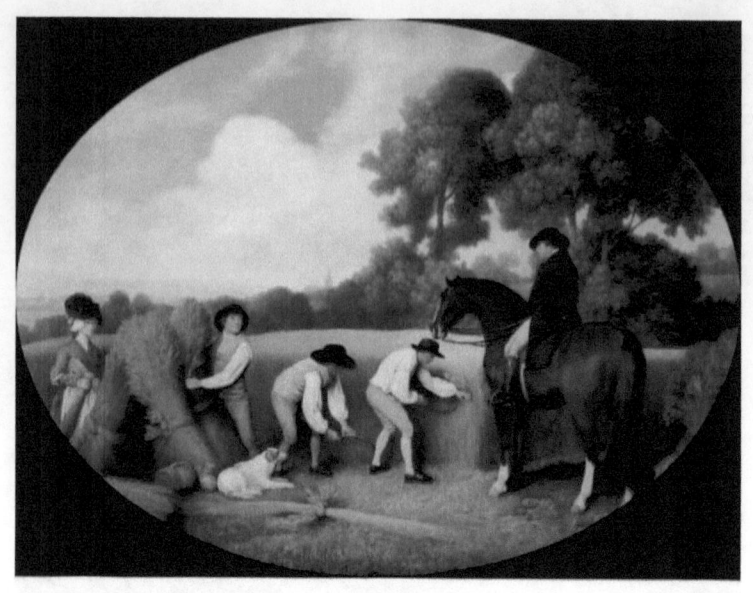

Reapers, 1795, oil

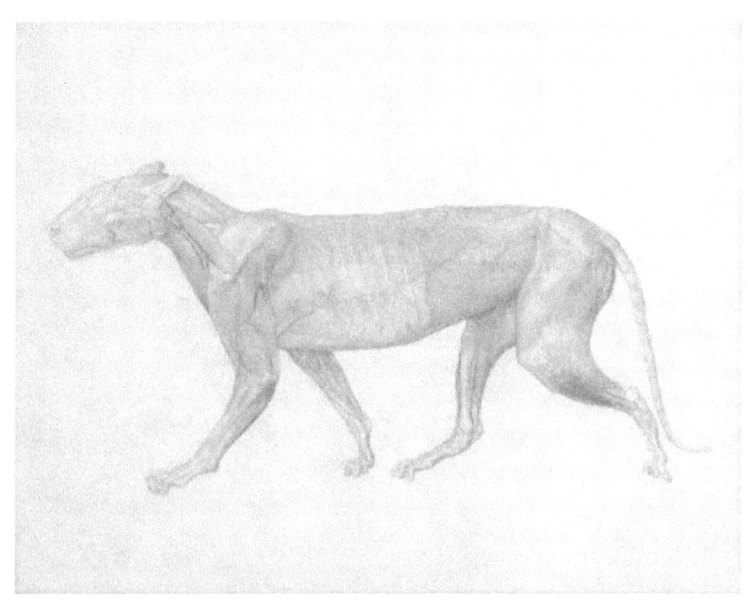

A Comparative Anatomical Exposition of the Structure
of the Human Body with that of a Tiger and a Common
Fowl, 1795-1806, drawing

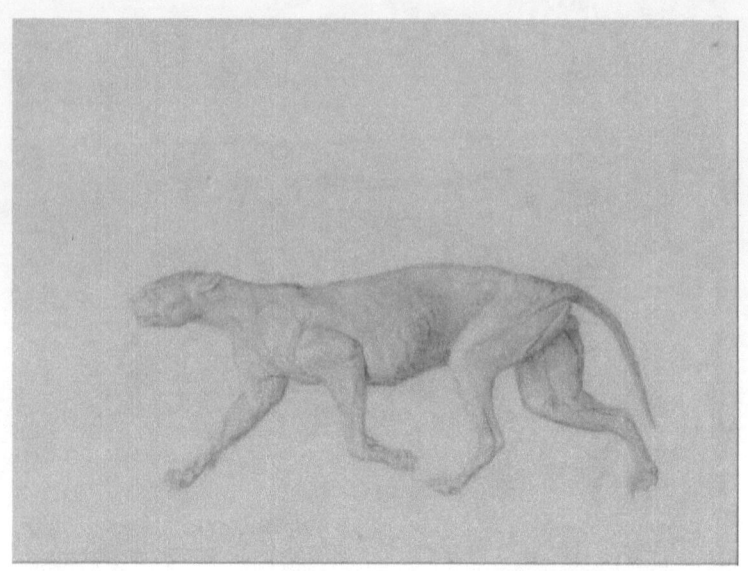

A Comparative Anatomical Exposition of the Structure
of the Human Body with That of a Tiger and a
Common Fowl: Leopard Body, 1795-1806, drawing

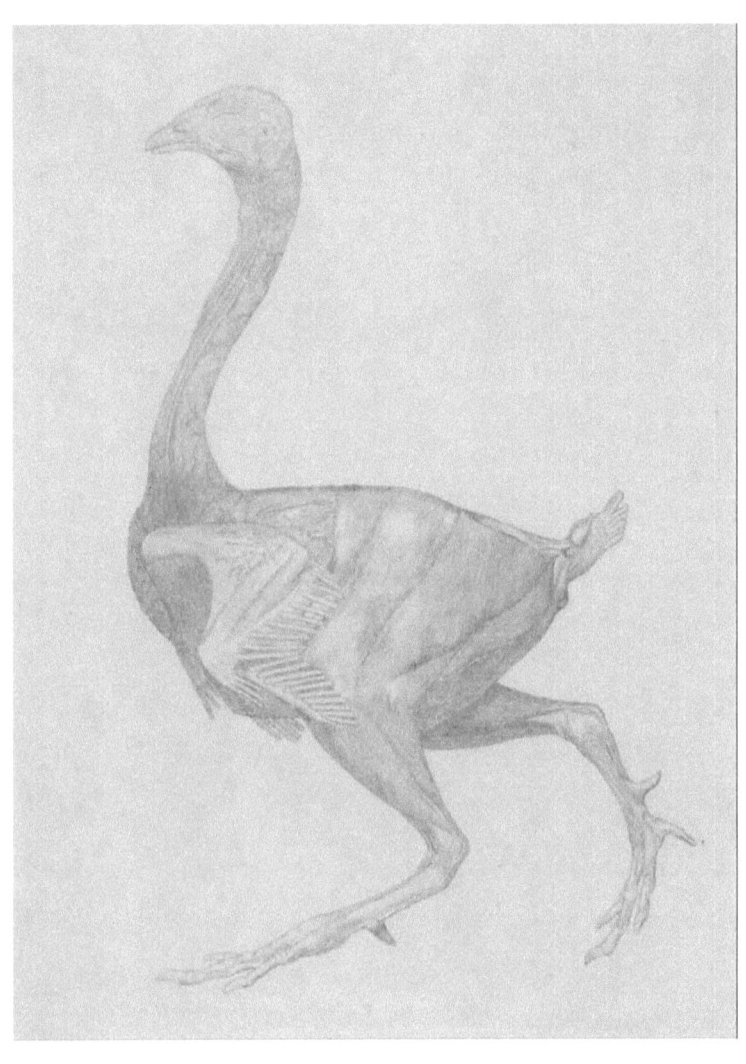

A Comparative Anatomical Exposition of the Structure
of the Human Body with That of a Tiger and a
Common Fowl: Fowl Body, 1795-1806, drawing

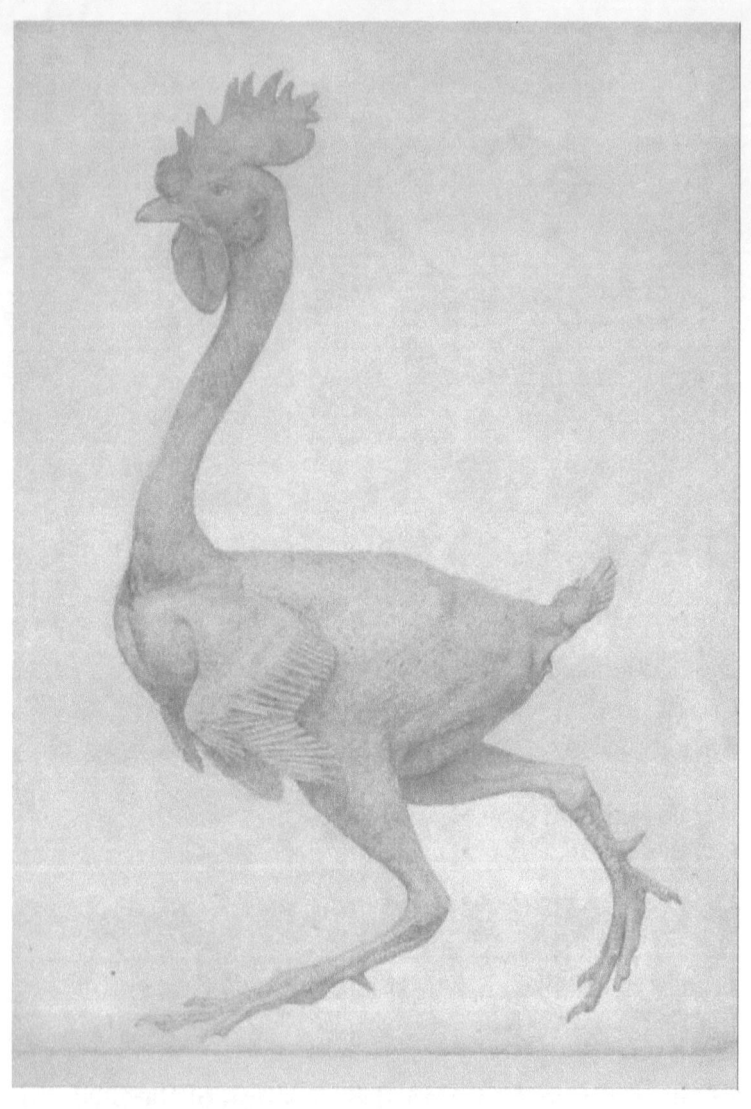

A Comparative Anatomical Exposition of the Structure
of the Human Body with that of a Tiger and a Common
Fowl: Fowl, 1795-1806, drawing

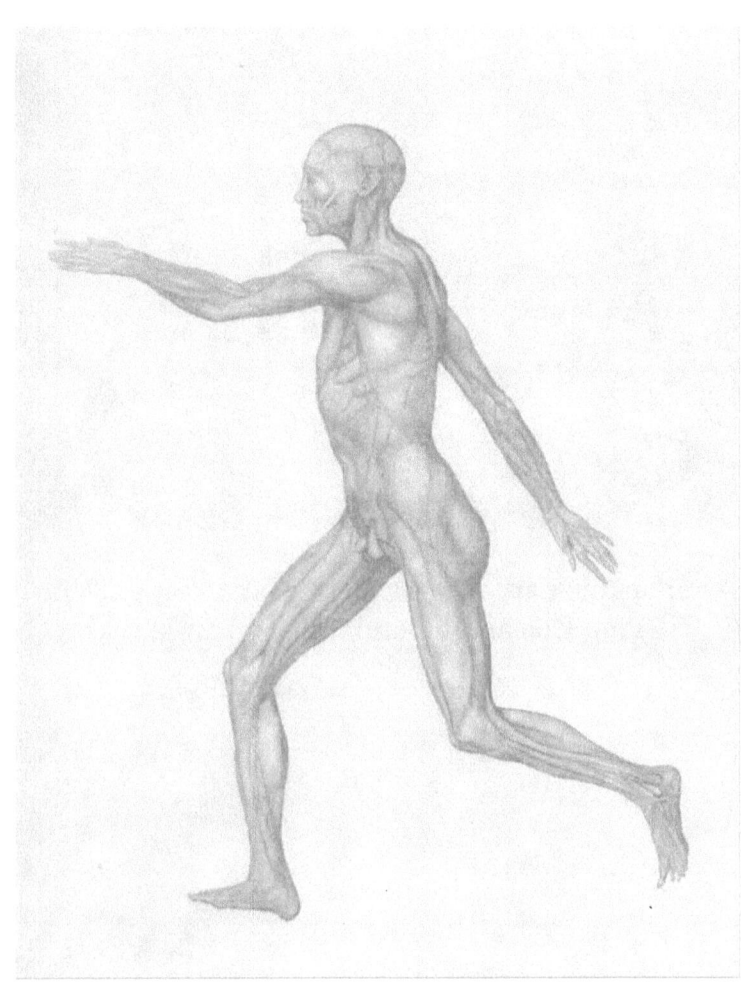

A Comparative Anatomical Exposition of the Structure of the Human Body with That of a Tiger and a Common Fowl: Human Figure, 1795-1806, drawing

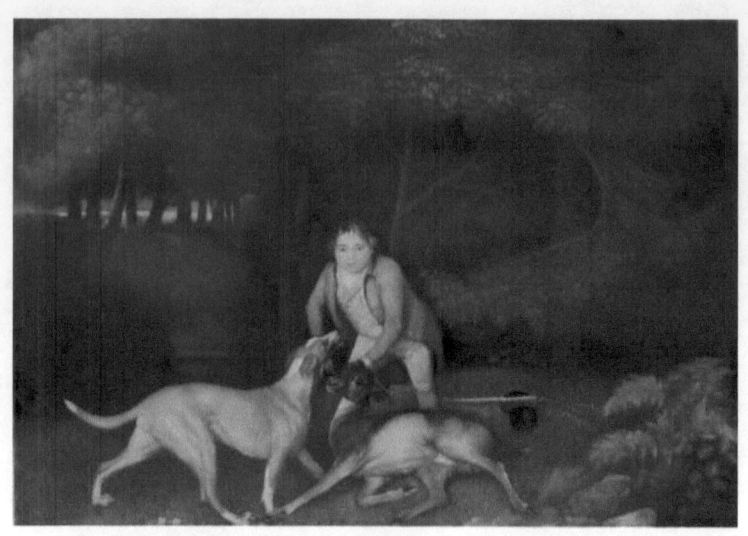

Freeman, the Earl of Clarendon's Gamekeeper, With a
Dying Doe and Hound, 1800, oil on canvas

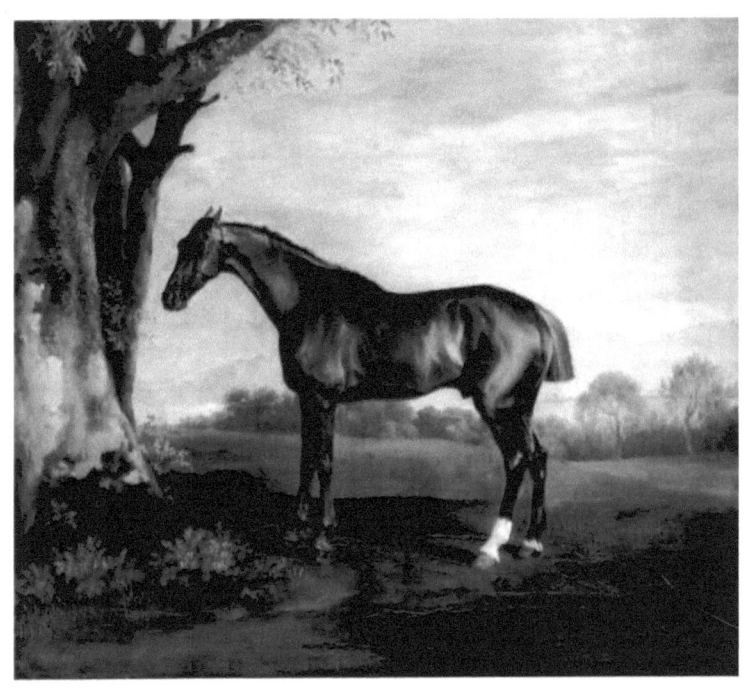

A Chestnut Racehorse, oil on canvas

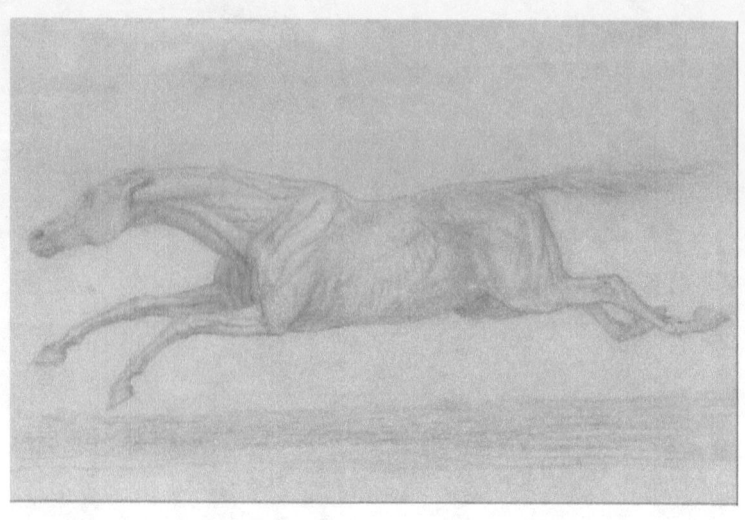

Study of a Racehorse in Action: Galloping to Left, a Semi-Anatomical Study, with Skin Flayed to Show Action of Muscles, drawing

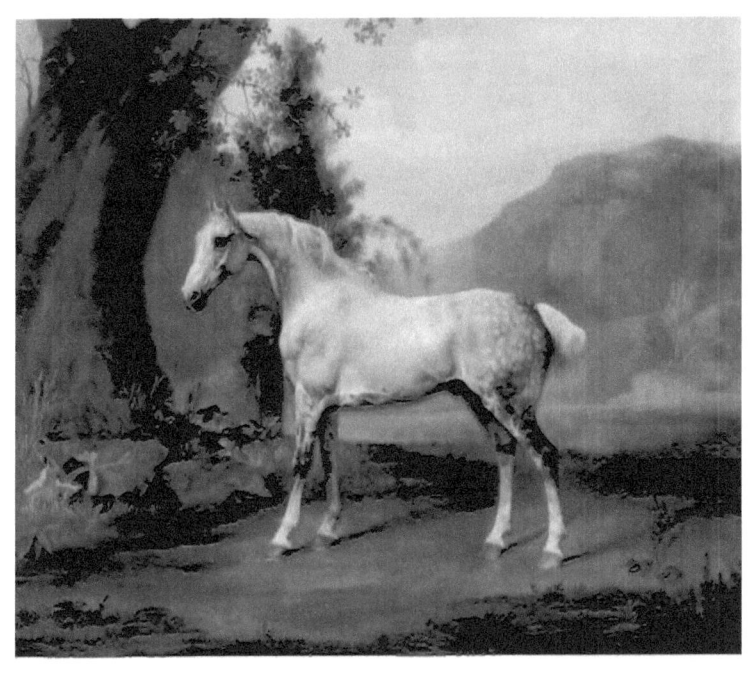

A Grey Stallion in a Landscape, oil on canvas

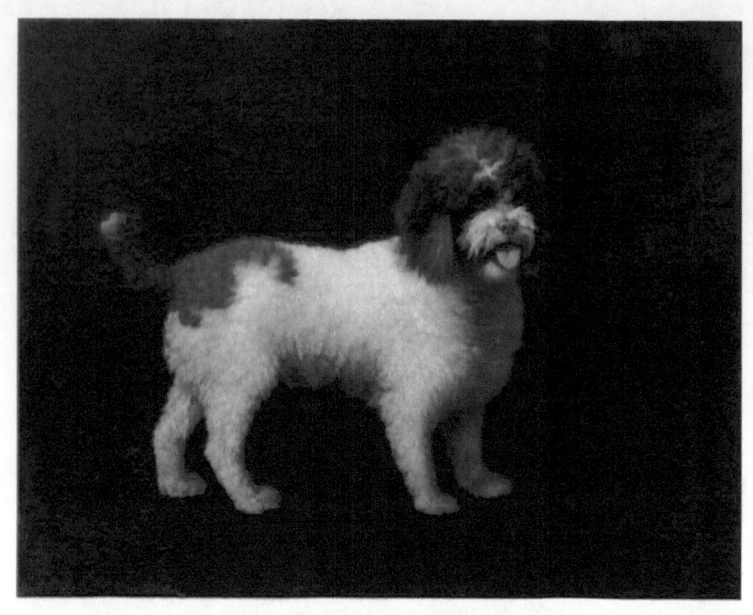

A Water Spaniel, oil on canvas

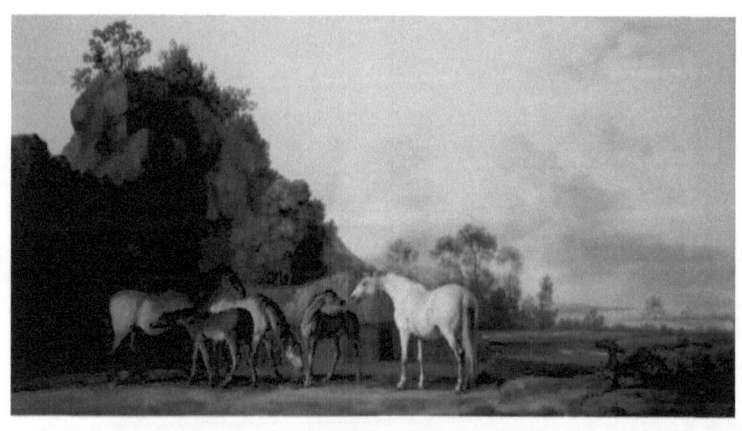

Brood Mares and Foals, oil on canvas

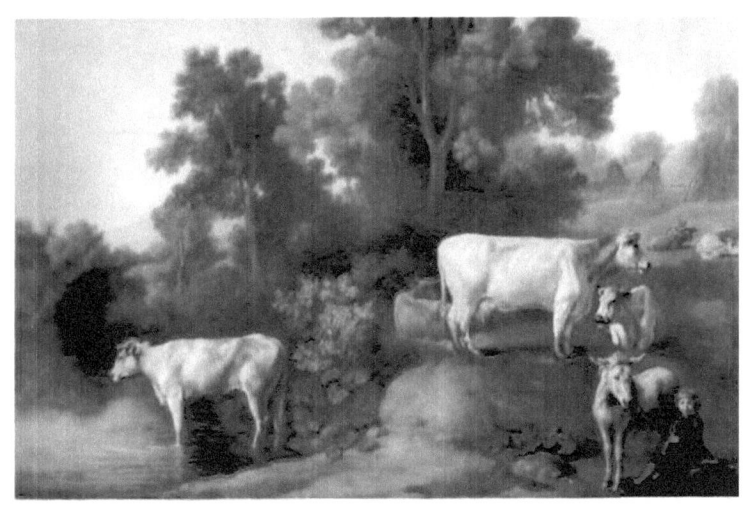

Cattle by a Stream, oil on canvas

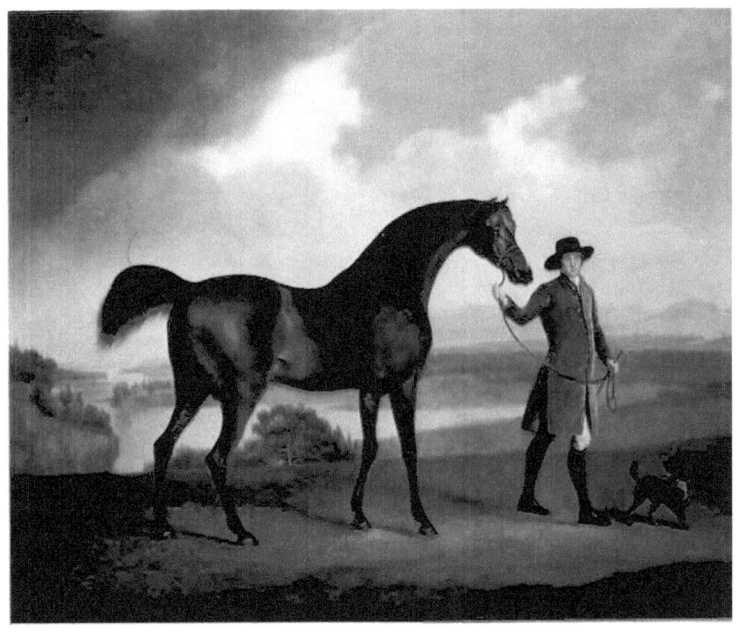

Earl Grosvenor's Bandy, oil on canvas

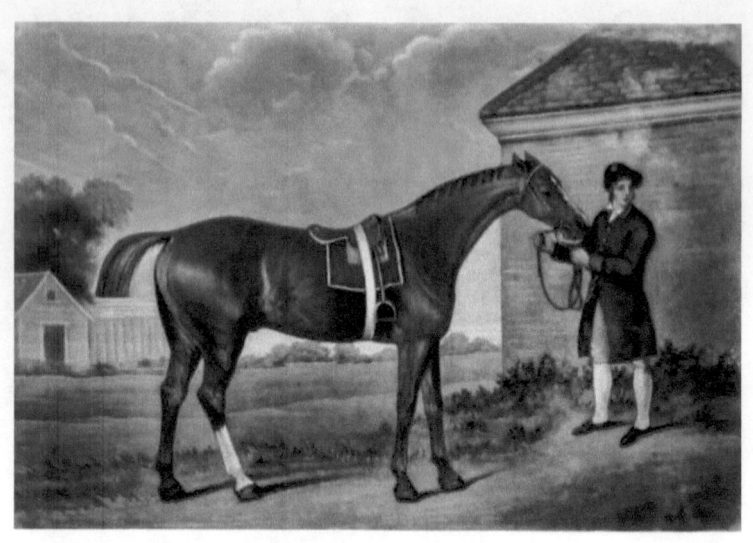

Eclipse, oil on canvas

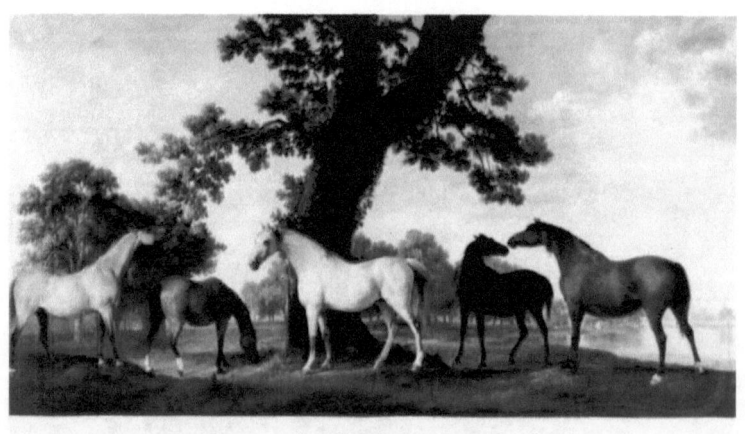

Five Brood Mares, oil on canvas

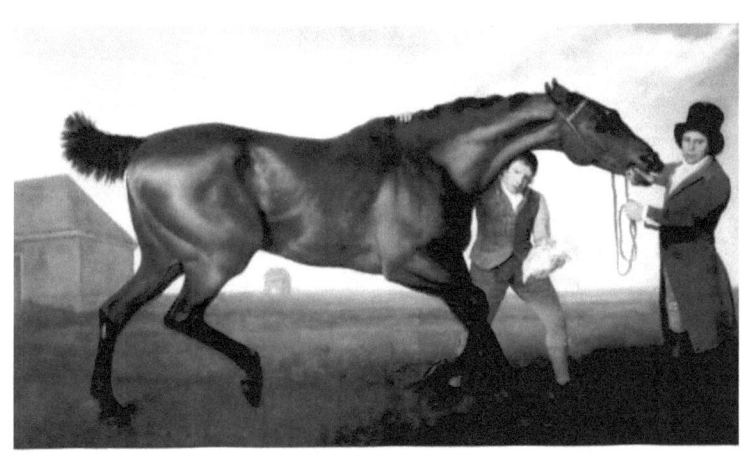

Hambletonian, oil on canvas

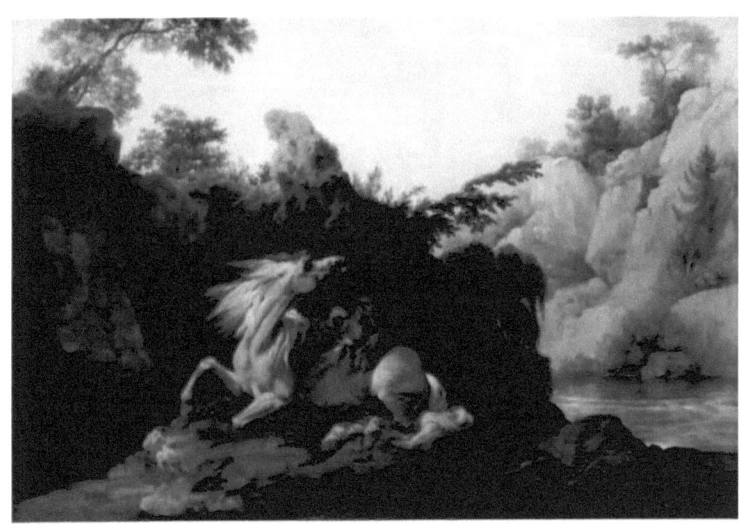

Horse Devoured by a Lion, oil on canvas

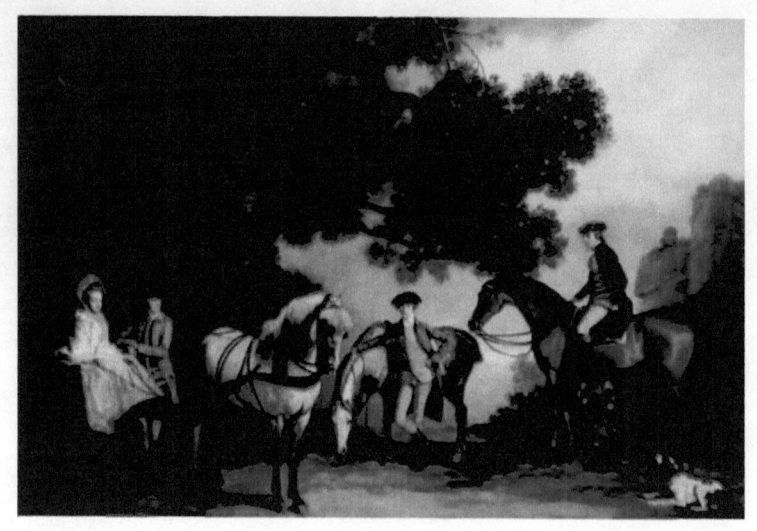

Melbourne and Milbanke Families, oil on canvas

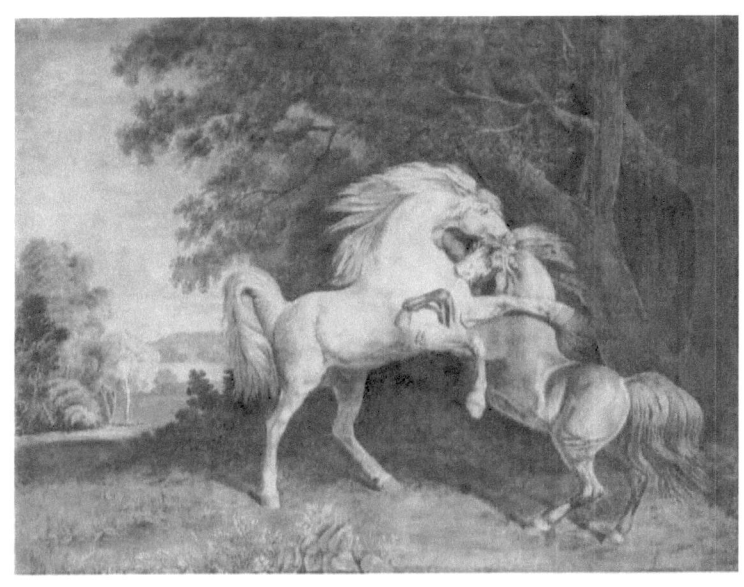

Horses Fighting, Watercolor, gouache, and pen and black ink on moderately thick, slightly textured, cream wove paper

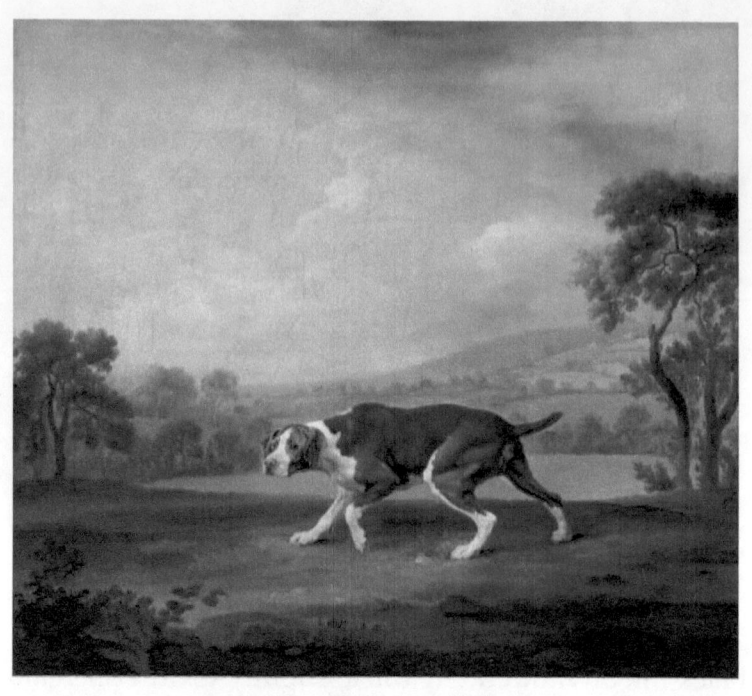

Spanish Pointer, oil on canvas

www.ingramcontent.com/pod-product-compliance
Lightning Source LLC
Chambersburg PA
CBHW021439170526
45164CB00001B/313